Codford
wool and war
in Wiltshire

An England's Past for Everyone paperback

Heritage Lottery Fund

VICTORIA
COUNTY
HISTORY

Institute of Historical
Research

Codford
wool and war
in Wiltshire

JOHN CHANDLER

with contributions from Matthew Bristow, Carrie Smith, Alan Thacker,
Sally Thomson, Dorothy Treasure and Elizabeth Williamson

Phillimore

First published 2007

A Victoria County History publication
Published by Phillimore & Co. Ltd, Shopwyke Manor Barn, Chichester, West
Sussex, England in association with the Institute of Historical Research at the
University of London.
www.phillimore.co.uk

ISBN 978-1-86077-441-6

British Library Cataloguing in Publication Data. A cataloguing record for this
book is available from the British Library.

Typeset in Humanist 521 and Minion

We wish particularly to thank the following EPE and VCH staff for their efforts
during the production of this volume:

John Beckett – Director of the Victoria County History
Matthew Bristow – Historic Environment Research Manager
Catherine Cavanagh – Project Manager
Nafisa Gaffar – Finance and Contracts Officer
Aretha George – Education and Skills Manager
Mel Hackett – Communications Officer
Stephen Lubell – Production and Editorial Controller
Neil Penlington – Administrator
Andrew Stokes – Web Manager
Alan Thacker – Executive Editor of the Victoria County History
Elizabeth Williamson – Architectural Editor of the Victoria County History

Printed and bound in Great Britain

Contents

List of Panels:

Preface

England's Past for Everyone (EPE) is a new venture by the Victoria County History. The VCH, as it is known, was established in 1899, and for over a century has been internationally recognised as one of the greatest publishing projects in English local history. EPE represents a new way of working for the VCH, bringing together professional historians and volunteers, to peel back the layers of our history and present their findings through paperback books, interactive websites, and projects for schools.

EPE has been made possible by a generous grant from the Heritage Lottery Fund to the Institute of Historical Research, which hosts the VCH, and by the support of our partners around the country. Fifteen projects are due to be completed between 2005 and 2010. Each one is designed to make local history available to new audiences, and to involve local people in its generation. Some are studies of individual places, whether villages or cities, some are mainly about individual buildings, some cover a diverse range of communities, and some relate to themes such as ethnicity and religion. But in essence, they are about good local history, studied from the original sources – documents, landscapes and buildings – and presented in words and images.

Through books, websites and a variety of learning materials, EPE hopes both to inform and to inspire – to inform our readers about places and people in the past, and to inspire them to undertake further work and to find out more about the places in which they live, or in which they are simply interested.

www.EnglandsPastForEveryone.org.uk
www.VictoriaCountyHistory.ac.uk

Professor John Beckett
Director of the Victoria County History

Foreword

This book focuses on the history of a single parish, albeit a somewhat unusual one in that it was formed from twin parishes only formally united in the 20th century. Readers may wonder why we should study the past at such a local level. Ultimately, it is because everywhere is unique, and no two places share the same history. It is the differences that make local history endlessly fascinating. Personalities, the vagaries of landscape, strokes of good fortune or disaster, human frailties and aspirations – all have contributed to the mix. We have sought in this book to bring out something of these particularities and at the same time to place them within the wider context of regional and national events.

But even if every place is unique and demands a unique response to its past, its historian must nevertheless have a method, like the chemist analysing a compound, or the detective unravelling a crime. Like any craftsman, we must understand the tools and materials of our trade. We hope that this book will introduce the reader to the ways in which the history of a parish can be investigated and the kinds of resources he or she might use. If, while reading about Codford's history, you have glanced at the endnotes which support the text, you will have sampled the range of sources which underpin our comprehension of a single parish. We have also interspersed the main narrative with panels, which illustrate how you might approach particular problems or points of special interest.

The book is complemented by an interactive website which allows you to explore relevant images, documents and audio visual material and which can be searched by people, places and themes. We keep putting up material as we discover it at www. EnglandsPastForEveryone.org.uk/Wiltshire.

Alongside the paperback and website, EPE worked with Wylye Valley School in Codford on an ambitious and successful undertaking to illustrate developments in local agriculture from earliest times to the present day. Activities included field, trips, writing in Latin, role play, and building a life-size Iron Age hut in the school grounds, complete with camp fire.

This entire enterprise has been very much a team effort. At its core lies research and writing carried out in 2003 by Carrie Smith, then Assistant Editor of VCH Wiltshire. The book itself has been produced by Wiltshire historian and local publisher, John

Chandler, with the EPE team based at the VCH London office, Elizabeth Williamson, Matthew Bristow and myself. Sally Thomson and Dorothy Treasure contributed additional material and worked with local volunteers including the Wiltshire Buildings Record.

The whole undertaking has been a happy and constructive one and we hope that you will find the results as rewarding as working on it has been for its contributors.

Alan Thacker
Executive Editor, VCH

Introducing Codford

The heart of the Wiltshire village of Codford lies along the lush Wylye Valley, sheltered by the stark edge of Salisbury Plain to the north and the chalk escarpments of the West Wiltshire Downs to the south. Most travellers on the A36 between Warminster and Salisbury, while delighting in the quiet beauty of the landscape that inspired Anthony Trollope in his novel the *Vicar of Bullhampton*, published in 1870, will take the bypass through the southern edge of the parish without giving Codford further thought. Yet, for those that care not only to leave the bypass but also wander from the main road through the village, Codford's history is revealed in its landscape, streets and buildings.

Codford and its surroundings are not only outstandingly beautiful, they are also rich in history. The modern parish, created only in 1934, lies in an area that was of great importance from

Figure 1 Codford in the Wylye Valley. A view from the south-west with Salisbury Plain to the north. The valley's 'special charm' was praised by the naturalist W.H. Hudson.

Figure 2 The county of Wiltshire in the SW of England.

earliest times. Only 10 miles or so from Stonehenge, it contains an important monument from the early Iron Age and, in the early Middle Ages, it lay at the heart of the West Saxon kingdom, among the rich estates of the Wylye Valley, focused on settlements such as Stockton, Sherrington and Chitterne. Codford, on the routeway connecting the royal centres of Wilton and Warminster, was first mentioned in a land grant made in 901 by King Alfred's son Edward the Elder; its famous and beautiful Anglo-Saxon sculpture bears witness to the sophisticated tastes of the local élite of that period (see Chapters 1 and 2).

Codford's history has been dominated by the twin influences of road and river. While it owes its origins to fords which crossed the Wylye at the point where the Chitterne brook runs into it, its later development has been largely determined by its proximity to the major routeway which runs south-eastwards along the river valley from Warminster to Salisbury, with the Salisbury Plain escarpment on its left and the river on its right. Its twin settlements of Codford St Mary and Codford St Peter, each with its own parish church, grew up beside this road – a road which at first benefited and latterly tormented them. By contrast the hamlet of Ashton Gifford, now simply a 19th-century country estate with house and park, lay secluded from the road, close to the river (Chapter 2). This river has been both beautiful and useful in Codford itself and in the neighbouring parishes along the valley. From around 1635 until the 19th century, it was managed to enrich the local pastures by means of an elaborate and ingenious system of channels which 'floated' (i.e. flooded) the riverside meadows every year to encourage the earlier growth of grass for grazing (see Chapter 4).[1]

Figure 3 The bridge carries Hindon Lane across the River Wylye, probably near the site of the original 'Coda's ford', and thus connects Codford St Mary with Stockton. It was built between 1759 and 1773.

Codford, meaning 'the ford of Coda', is first mentioned in 901. We do not know anything more about the Coda who gave his name to the ford or about the settlement which grew up beside it, but it seems likely that at that time the entire area of the present parish was a single estate. Only later was it formed into two separate parishes – Codford St Mary and Codford St Peter. Although it is not known when the estate came thus to be divided, it cannot have been later than the 12th century, as by the earlier 11th century there were already at least three settlements – the two Codfords and Ashton, which also has an Anglo-Saxon name, meaning 'ash-tree farm'. 'Gifford' was added later to distinguish the village from other Ashtons nearby, and derives from the name of the family which held it in the 13th century (see Chapter 3).[2]

Present-day Codford was formed from the gradual coalescence of two of Codford's medieval settlements, each grouped around its own parish church. Near those two churches, the earliest and most interesting buildings in the village, lie several of the oldest and most important houses – rectories and ancient farms. Most of today's settlement lies along the High Street, the old main road running slightly south-eastwards from Codford St Peter to the bridge over the Chitterne brook in Codford St Mary. Old buildings, many of them originally farms, make attractive groups round St Peter's church and at the east end of High Street and towards St Mary's church. Like most of the houses built between the wooded Wylye Valley and the chalky hills they are built in a rich mixture of local materials – timber and thatch, rubbly limestone, flint and chalk, and brick. Later buildings grew up in the centre of the village between the two earliest groups. Many of them, such as the Congregationalists' former manse and school, are 19th century, and some that look modern are much older behind (see Chapter 2). The 19th century gave Codford one of West Wiltshire's most interesting industrial groups – the tall brick and stone Woolstore, built together with neighbouring Wool House and cottages by a local entrepreneur, James Raxworthy (see Chapter 4).

Here are watered meadows nearest to the river on both sides; then the gardens, the houses, and the corn-fields. After the corn-fields come the downs; but, generally speaking, the downs are not so bold here as they are on the sides of the Avon.

William Cobbett, *Rural Rides*, 1826

Apart from the owners of an early 19th-century mansion at Ashton Gifford, Codford has had almost no resident gentry and until recent times local society was dominated by working farmers. Many were tenants of absentee landowners, some of whom, like the Mompessons of Codford St Mary, the Giffords and Mautravers of Codford St Peter, and the Talbots, earls of Shrewsbury, of Ashton Gifford, were important in the wider world (see Chapter 3). In common with neighbouring villages of the Wylye Valley, agriculture, principally sheep-rearing and the production of barley, has always been the dominant occupation. For much of recorded history this line carried on in open fields and common pastures until these were inclosed at the end of the 18th and in the earlier 19th centuries. Sheep had a key role. Grazed on the higher slopes of the downs by day, they were folded by night on the arable fields to manure them. The main industrial activity – weaving, spinning, fulling and, later, the sorting and grading of fleeces – has been based upon wool, originally local but later including much imported from elsewhere in the county or even further afield (see Chapter 4).

As elsewhere, the mechanisation of farming and the building of new houses, first for local people and then mainly for incomers, has transformed this agrarian community. Nevertheless, it still has a strong local identity. Much that characterised Codford in the 19th century is still there today. Worship according to the Anglican

Figure 5 The cap badge on the slope above Foxhole Bottom, made by Australian troops, 1916-17, incorporating glass beer bottle bases. Polishing the bottles became a punishment duty, giving rise to the site's colloquial name, 'Misery Hill'. Turfed over during the Second World War to prevent its use as a landmark by enemy bombers, the outline was restored in chalk and last scoured in 1999 by Australian troops.

liturgy is still offered in its two churches; its young children are still taught in its primary school; and it has a variety of sporting clubs and other leisure activities, including most notably its own small but complete Woolstore Theatre (see Panel 11).

Codford has not been at the centre of events, at least since the Norman Conquest, but it has enjoyed moments of great activity in the 20th century, particularly in relation to the two World Wars. Its vital contribution, well documented in print, remains etched on local memories. Codford's location on the edge of Salisbury Plain ensured that it was caught up in the great encampments of British and Commonwealth troops established there for training purposes in both World Wars. The troops' sojourn had an extraordinary, albeit temporary, effect on the character and appearance of the village. An Australian cap badge cut in downland chalk overlooking Codford and the Wylye Valley is a permanent memorial of the ANZAC contribution to this remarkable episode, a contribution still commemorated every year at the ANZAC cemetery in the parish (see Chapter 7).

Codford might be described as a quintessentially English parish, and like every parish it has its own story to tell. *Codford: Wool and War in Wiltshire* describes how a small settlement on the edge of Salisbury Plain has evolved, why its landscape and buildings look as they do, and how its people, their livelihoods and social connections have made it what it is. We hope that our readers will enjoy Codford's story and find something that resonates with their own experience of English places.

Figure 6 Codford from
the south-east, seen from
a hot air balloon in 2002.
The village, clustered
along the high street,
lies in the valley with the
A36 bypass to its south,
revealing the agricultural
and downland character
of Codford's landscape.

Chapter 1

Land and Settlers

THE LAND ITSELF

The river, naturally, is the lowest part of the parish, here some 100 metres above sea level. From the valley the land rises, gently at first, and then north of the village more steeply up on to the downs. On both sides of the Chitterne brook the terrain is relatively flat, but between the folds and spurs of downland there are steep hillsides, especially leading up to Codford Hill, which at 188 metres is the highest point in the parish. One such slope, above Foxhole Bottom, displays the Australian cap badge, while Codford Hill itself is crowned by an Iron-Age enclosure, now known as Codford Circle. The highest points around the parish edge are Clay Pit Hill (178 metres) and along the western boundary with Upton Lovell (165 metres).

Codford's bedrock is chalk (see Map 4). Never far below the surface it is mantled by thin, dry and relatively poor soils, except where strips of alluvium and river gravel have accumulated alongside the Chitterne brook, and in the valley from the Wylye as far up as the main road. It is a treeless landscape, apart from some small 19th-century plantations, although the familiar open downland scenery belies the likelihood that it results from forest clearance during the Neolithic and Bronze Ages.[3]

The richer soils of the valley pastures are suitable for rearing cattle but, until artificial fertilisers were introduced in the 19th century, corn growing in Codford was a thankless task, its chalky soils needing constant enrichment from livestock, above all the common flocks of sheep. Here as elsewhere the technique was to lay out open arable fields on the more fertile lower slopes and dry or tributary valleys. At Codford by the 11th century, arable fields probably extended across the valley of the Chitterne brook and up the slopes beyond. The floating of water meadows alongside the Wylye from the 17th century onwards encouraged more productive and flexible husbandry, and an increase in cattle (see Panel 9). But sheep and corn farming continued to be the dominant form of agriculture well into the 20th century, and Manor Farm retained its flock until 2002. The water meadows are neglected now, and have reverted to tussocky marshland, partly as a result of dredging the river in the mid-20th century. Arable farming now predominates in the parish.[4]

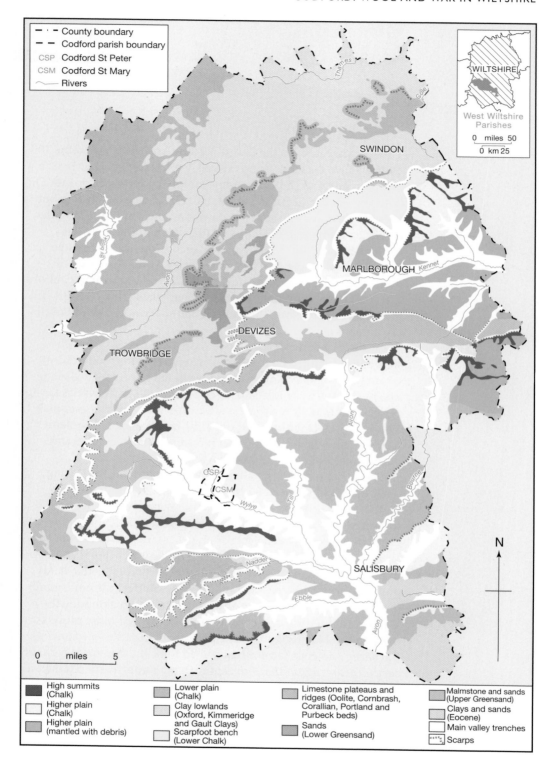

Map 1 (left) Map of Wiltshire showing solid geology and highlighting the location of Codford St Mary and Codford St Peter.

LIVING HERE

Early Settlement

What was to become Codford's downland formed part of a much larger prehistoric landscape extending across Salisbury Plain above the Wylye Valley. Our evidence for the nature of that landscape, and the human activity which shaped it, is necessarily extremely limited, since without written sources we are wholly dependent on (usually piecemeal) archaeological discoveries or interpretations of surviving man-made features. The landscape of which Codford formed a part was managed for arable cultivation, and characterised by extensive areas of small rectilinear and interconnecting

Map 2 Parish map showing contours.

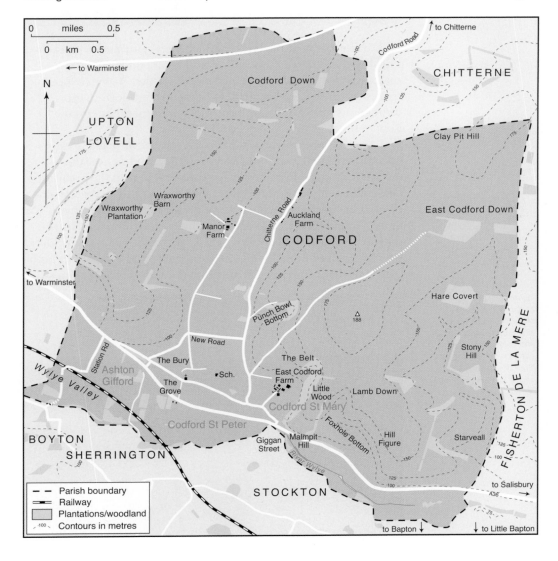

Figure 7 The ford, Codford St Mary, crossed by timber footbridge and 18th-century stone bridge.

fields. Faint traces of the banks and lynchets associated with such a field system survive. Codford's examples are undated, but by analogy with systems investigated elsewhere they may have been created as early as the Neolithic period and continued in use throughout the Bronze and Iron Ages, and sometimes into the Roman times.

A number of enclosures have been identified as possible early upland settlement sites or farmsteads. One such lies near the modern Chitterne Road and may be associated with the prehistoric fields, although it cannot be dated. Another, a C-shaped enclosure close to the north-eastern corner of the later parish, identified by aerial photography, has been interpreted as a Romano-British settlement. The site itself must be later than the prehistoric fields in which it is located since it cuts across their boundaries, but its occupants may have continued farming on the earlier pattern. Finds

Figure 8 Lamb Down, east of Codford, a chalk downland rich in prehistoric monuments and finds of flint and early metalwork. Many monuments are still visible on the ground or in aerial photographs.

Figure 9 Codford Circle, with its bank and ditch, viewed from the air looking south, with Punch Bowl Bottom to the right. In the middle distance St Mary's Church and East Farm with the village to their right. Further south the river Wylye and the downland above Sherrington, clothed partly in extensive woodland along Great Ridge.

at Manor Farm suggest that it too may have originated as an early farmstead. Nevertheless, it remains possible that the majority of the prehistoric and Roman inhabitants, like their successors, lived not on the downs but below in the valley, all trace of their occupation having been obliterated by later farming and settlement.[5]

The parish's most important prehistoric monument probably dates from the early Iron Age. The hilltop enclosure known as Codford Circle lies on a high spur of downland overlooking modern Codford and contains unusual evidence of human activity (see Panel 1). Rather older are two groups of Bronze Age barrows, on Lamb Down in the east of the parish and in Ashton Valley on the northern downland. Several barrows were investigated in the 19th century and some have been re-examined since. They were found to contain cremations and grave-goods, including axes and an urn. One had been reused during the Iron Age. Otherwise evidence of prehistoric life on the uplands has been traced only through stray finds which include a Neolithic axe from Starveall, Neolithic pottery sherds and flint on Lamb Down, a Bronze Age socketed axe and an Iron Age brooch from Manor Farm, and three pre-Roman coins, including one from Carthage, dated *c*.146 BC.[6]

Evidence of Romano-British activity in Codford is meagre. The C-shaped enclosure, already discussed, has yielded pottery sherds, fragments of a corn-drying oven, an iron sickle and a fourth-century silver coin. In addition two other possible habitation sites on Malmpit Hill have been found, together with stray finds of coins and brooches from various locations, including Manor Farm and the bypass construction.[7]

Codford Circle

Standing sentinel over the Wessex chalklands and their valleys are prehistoric enclosures, generally referred to as hillforts. Some, such as Battlesbury and Scratchbury, further up the Wylye Valley, are massive and formidable and clearly could have had a military and defensive purpose. Many others, however, are more modest and are perhaps more likely to have had functions connected with agriculture, ritual or display. One such hilltop enclosure, which has had a bewildering variety of names – Oldbury, Oldborough, Woolborough, Yarnbury, Wilsbury, Codford Camp and Codford Castle – surmounts Malmpit Hill, on the spur of downland north-east of Codford St Mary village.

Evidence from sites which have been excavated has led scholars to think that such enclosures date from the Iron Age. But the reality is often more complex. At Codford, an aerial photograph revealed cropmarks within the extant single bank and ditch, consistent with a much earlier type of monument, a Neolithic cause-wayed enclosure. An archaeological investigation was therefore conducted in 2001. The work was directed by Drs Michael Allen and Julie Gardiner, both eminent prehistorians and Codford residents, and many local people participated as excavators.

A section cut through the bank and ditch revealed that, although the bank had never been very high, the ditch was originally a substantial feature – over 5 metres wide and 2.2 metres deep. The two crop-marks were found to have been produced by pits, one of which was fully excavated. Cut into the solid chalk to a depth of 3 metres and measuring 2 x 3 metres across, it contained a dark sticky deposit comprising charcoal, burnt flint, burnt or charred animal bones and a small, scorched sarsen boulder. This material, which has been interpreted as deliberately dumped food waste, something akin to the residue of a large prehistoric barbeque, was covered over soon after it had been placed in the pit. All the datable finds suggest that the pit and its deposit belong to the early Iron Age rather than the Neolithic period. Nothing comparable has been found in other similar hilltop enclosures.

A later ground survey, conducted in 2005 by Dr David Field of English Heritage, again with the assistance of local residents, confirmed the cropmarks and showed the presence of a potentially earlier non-defensive inner ditch circuit. Further investigations are planned.

Sources: This information has been supplied by Dr Mike Allen. More information can be found in 'Codford Circle: Iron Age Pits and Feasting', in *Past: the Newsletter of the Prehistoric Society*, No. 53, July 2006. This is available online at http: //ucl. ac.uk/prehistoric/

The Fords and the Early Estates

By the early Middle Ages, if not before, the Wylye Valley had become an important routeway. Codford was sited on an ancient road running on the north side of the river, from Warminster in the west to Wilton in the east. It grew up on that road at the point at which the Chitterne brook, which flowed down from the north side of the valley, joined the main river. In Anglo-Saxon times, if not before, two fords were located there. One, presumably the more important, was Coda's ford, from which as we have seen the village derives its name, while the second was known as Odenford or Oda's ford. Later changes to the courses of the river and the brook, caused by the construction of water meadows have made it difficult to locate precisely the sites of these fords. Early documentary evidence shows, however, that both crossed the Wylye itself and not the lesser stream. Almost certainly, they lay close to the confluence of brook and river.

As we shall see in a moment, in Anglo-Saxon times this part of the Wylye Valley formed an important area of planned estates, and the two fords lay on routes connecting Codford with two neighbouring estate centres. Coda's ford probably formed part of the route south across the Wylye, along the line of today's Hindon Lane, from Codford to the early manorial centre of Stockton. Oda's ford seems to have lain very close but a little to the west, on the line of today's Giggan Street, and carried a route leading south-west to another early manorial centre, Sherrington, which lay to the west of Stockton. The boundaries of all three estates probably came together at the fords.[8]

A lesser routeway ran northwards from the two settlements on either side of the Chitterne brook, to Chitterne, another manorial centre. The main route was probably always that which lay to the east of the brook, known today as the Chitterne road, connecting Chitterne with Codford St Mary.

The earliest documentary reference to Coda's ford tells us that, in the reign of King Alfred (871–899), it lay on that section of the river Wylye which formed the northern edge of the important estate of Stockton. Stockton had belonged to a high official, Ealdorman Wulfhere, but had been forfeited by him for desertion, presumably during Alfred's wars against the invading Danes. At that time, as the shared name suggests, the whole of the area covered by the two later parishes of Codford may, like Stockton, have been a single estate. Like the neighbouring parishes on both sides of the Wylye, that area is roughly rectangular and arranged on an axis running north-east to south-west (see Map 4). Currently covering some 1,534 hectares – almost unchanged since the Early

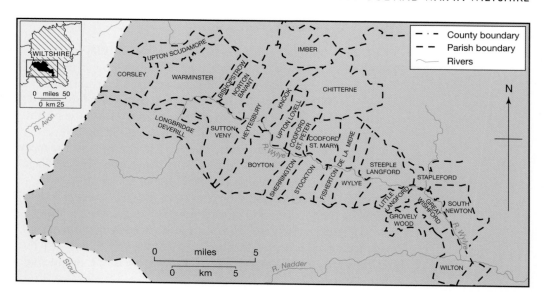

Map 3 **Map 3** The Wylye Valley between Warminster and Wilton, showing planned development of parishes.

Middle Ages – it is much the same size as Stockton and Boyton, also nearby. A similar form of layout dominates the whole of the Wylye Valley, the boundaries of both parishes and lesser divisions such as tithings forming more or less rectangular strips running from the high chalkland down to the river (see Chapter 5). Both Codford parishes have this form, as well as Codford as a whole. Significantly, the only natural feature determining their boundaries is the all-important river, which forms their south-western side and the Chitterne brook which divides them. (See Map 3).

The regularity of these arrangements suggests that they were man-made, the product of planning. They seem to be part of a reorganisation of territories, which eventually included the laying out of open fields on the valley sides and the establishment of village settlements between those fields and the riverside meadows. Dated boundary charters show that this pattern had been achieved by the late Anglo-Saxon period in much of the valley. It may already have been well under way when we first hear of Codford in 901.[9]

We do not know when the putative original unitary estate or territory of Codford became divided into the two parishes of Codford St Peter and Codford St Mary. Undoubtedly this had happened before the mid-12th century, by which time the two churches were in existence (see Chapter 2 and Chapter 6). Probably indeed it was before 1066, when the area was divided into three estates corresponding to the three settlements of Codford St Mary, Codford St Peter and Ashton (see Chapter 3). As we have seen, topographical factors probably played a part in this division; north

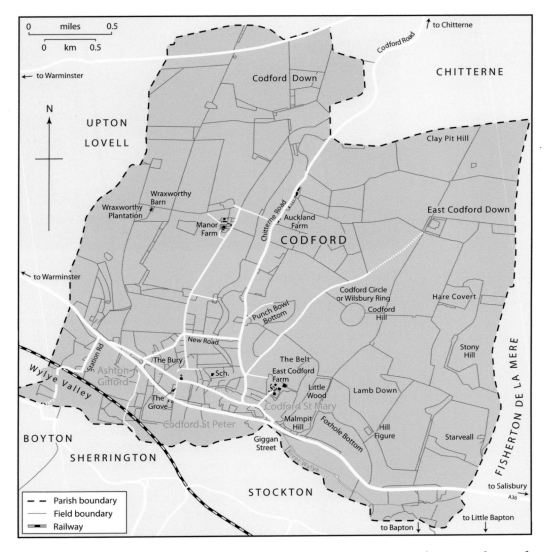

Map 4 Parish map showing post-enclosure field boundaries.

of the High Street, the two parishes lie respectively west and east of the Chitterne brook.

Codford St Mary had been the larger of the two and remained a single estate. Codford St Peter, however, was already divided into two estates by 1066 and thereafter was divided into three. Of these, the westernmost, Ashton Gifford, became a separate administrative unit known as a tithing (see Chapter 5). Ashton's ragged eastern boundary with Codford suggests that it was drawn to take account of open-field strips already in being. The present Green Lane may have formed the boundary between the two estates comprising the remainder of Codford St Peter.[10]

Figure 10 The 18th-century bridge carrying High Street over the Chitterne Brook in Codford St Mary.

The Codfords Take Shape

We know little of the nature of settlement within these early medieval estates; all archaeological traces are likely to have been obliterated by centuries of later occupation. At some point, however, the prehistoric downland landscape of scattered farmsteads or hamlets was transformed into one of compact villages, a process probably initiated by landowners to make agricultural production more efficient. At Codford, as elsewhere, the transformation may have begun as early as the 9th century and was almost certainly well under way in the late Anglo-Saxon period. The emergence of three estate centres by 1066 suggests that Codford St Mary, Codford St Peter and Ashton Gifford, the three separate villages from which modern Codford has evolved, were already in being.

The late Anglo-Saxon settlements at Codford St Peter and Codford St Mary probably clustered around the churches. Codford St Peter, which lay on the main road and has an Anglo-Saxon

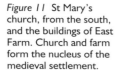

Figure 11 St Mary's church, from the south, and the buildings of East Farm. Church and farm form the nucleus of the medieval settlement.

sculptured stone of exceptional quality dating from the late eighth
or early ninth century, was perhaps the earlier, perhaps even
the centre of the ancient unitary estate (see Panel 3). However,
apart from this stone, which forms part of a cross-shaft or of an
architectural feature flanking an opening, Codford's Anglo-Saxon
inhabitants have left few traces. Except for a few stray finds outside
the main settlement areas, in particular a silver coin and a stirrup
mount at Manor Farm, which may well have been an isolated early
farmstead, the only tangible relics of the period are some early
Anglo-Saxon grave goods from reused prehistoric barrows on the
downs in the north of the parish.[11]

Nevertheless, Anglo-Saxon Codford was not a negligible place.
As we have seen, it lay in the heartland of the kingdom of Wessex
in an area of ancient and stable royal estates. These estates were
assessed for the purposes of taxation in multiples of five hides,
units which in late Anglo-Saxon times were regarded as sufficient
to support an armed warrior, or thegn, and his household (see
Panel 6). In the time of King Edward the Confessor, before the
Norman Conquest, the two Codford parishes were the focus
of estates assessed for the purposes of taxation at 15 hides, that
is, as having sufficient resources to support three such warrior
households. Three lords are named, and although, as later, they
may well have been absentee, they presumably had estate centres at
Codford's three settlements. These resources compare favourably
with the royal estates of Stockton and Sherrington, each assessed at
10 hides in the 10th century, which suggests that the settlements at
the fords were by no means insignificant.[12]

Map 5 Map of 1773,
showing settlement
focused along the main
road between Codford
St Mary and Codford St
Peter.

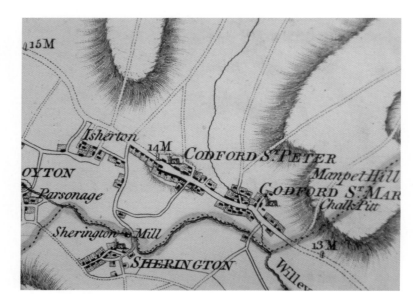

This view is supported by other evidence. In 1086 the most valuable of the Codford estates, Codford St Mary, was one of the principal holdings of Waleran the huntsman, a leading local landowner with property concentrated in Wiltshire and Dorset, whose task may have been to develop royal hunting forests in the south of the county. Although almost certainly he did not live there, Waleran kept the estate, which included a substantial home farm, in his own hands. Similarly, although it was considerably less valuable, Osbern Giffard kept direct control of his share of Codford St Peter. The quality and sophistication of the Anglo-Saxon carving at Codford St Peter suggests that by the early ninth century, as later, someone of wealth and importance had close links with Codford.

The church and chief house of Codford St Mary occupied a raised site, presumably less prone to flood, but commercial success depended on the passing trade to such a degree that from an early date much of the village was surely lower down, near or on the main road. The settlement may have had a fledgling market, which was recorded in a grant of 1254 but is otherwise unknown.[13] At Codford St Peter the original nucleus, perhaps a planned

Map 6 Enclosure Award map (1810) for Codford St Peter, showing the main area of settlement before the merging with St Mary.

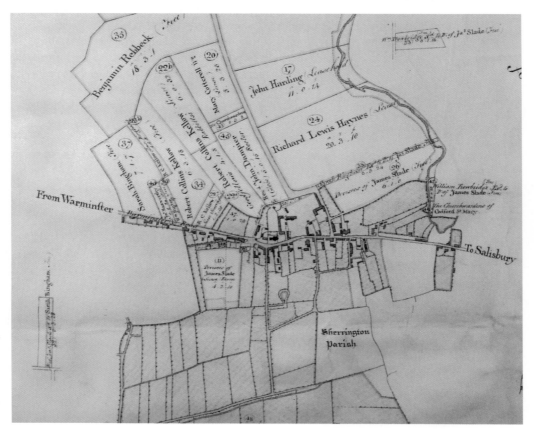

Figure 12 Church and chief house of Codford St Mary. Drawn by Buckler c.1804.

Figure 12 Church and chief house of Codford St Mary. Drawn by Buckler c.1804.

development of the late Anglo-Saxon period, seems to have been an approximate rectangle extending northwards from the main road, and including church, rectory and demesne farm. From this beginning the settlement spread along the main road.

Roads and Settlements

The pattern of roads, initially determined by downs and river, tells us something about how the settlements developed. The early pattern and how it was elaborated can be established to a reasonably certain degree by the use of historic maps, created of course much later than the earliest roads, and by the age of the buildings along the roads.[14]

The present-day High Street, part of a very old route between Wilton and Warminster, linked the two Codfords. As we have seen, the church and buildings associated with the manor of Codford St Peter were focused upon this road, whereas the church and chief house of the manor of Codford St Mary lay to the north, with the village perhaps originally clustered between them and the main road. A short stretch of another, perhaps an ancient east–west, route (now the B390) crosses the downs towards the northern edge of the parishes. The impact of this route, regarded in 1675 as part of the main route from London to North Devon, is unknown, but the name Anstlow Hill, in Knook one kilometre west of the Codford boundary, derives from an Anglo-Saxon word meaning 'pass' and suggests that the road was in use before the Norman conquest (see Map 5).[15]

Of the network of routes linking Codford with its neighbours and its farmland many, like Giggan Street and Green Lane, have long since dwindled to back lanes, footpaths and bridleways. A map of 1773 shows roads leading south across the valley to Boyton, Sherrington and Stockton, and north to Chitterne. To the south, Hindon Lane, until 1939 a privately owned toll road, led from Codford St Mary to Stockton, with Giggan Street branching off it to Sherrington. Boyton Lane ran from Codford St Peter through Ashton Gifford to Boyton, and from Ashton Gifford a track ran north to join the Chitterne to Heytesbury road. The roads or trackways, which led north from each Codford to Chitterne, were connected by a bridleway, known as Stordway, which ran eastwards from Green Lane (the road from Codford St Peter) to the Chitterne road (that from Codford St Mary). From there another way branched north-eastwards across the downs. [16]

The antiquity of the old main road is not in doubt, but Chitterne Road and Church Lane in Codford St Mary must also be old, as buildings of the 16th century survive or have been recorded along them. In contrast, Green Lane had few buildings and has none now, partly because its lower part was hemmed in on the west by the former rectory land, which the lane curves to avoid, and on the east by the inn and brewery; indeed the lane was sometimes known as George or Brewery Lane. The same lack of surviving early houses is true of Beanis Path and Cheapside, which run west from Church Lane as a footpath and back lane and may have been important parts of Codford St Mary's road network. Maps show that Cheapside once had more dwellings and so did the southern roads, even though water meadows and marshland prevented

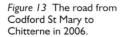

Figure 13 The road from Codford St Mary to Chitterne in 2006.

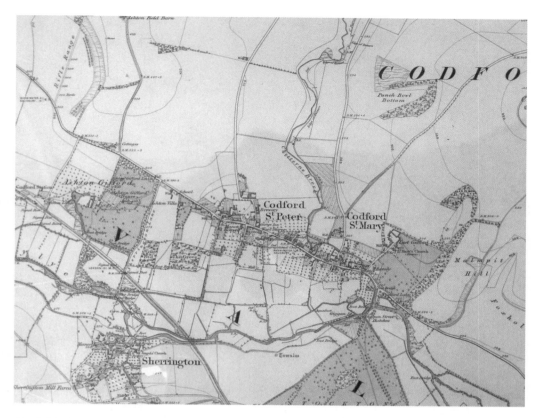

Map 7 The Codfords in 1886 showing the communication pattern.

much building. A lane in Codford St Mary that led to the river from the main road at a point west of Chitterne Road has gone, but traces of two other such roads – Crouch's Lane and Doughty's Lane or Frog Alley (which led to the water meadows) – survive in Codford St Peter.

The main road had already become the principal focus of settlement in Codford St Mary by the early 17th century, when there may have been as many as twenty houses spread along it. Thereafter it was to become more important still. A map of the 1760s shows that by then, apart from the East Farm complex and a few buildings along Church Lane, most premises either fronted the main road (on the north side) or abutted it end-on in rows (on the south side). Many of the houses along High Street survive, including about half a dozen of the 17th century. Most were built as farmhouses and still have barns behind them, some of which are later than the houses.[17]

A picture of the progress of Codford St Peter is given by two manorial surveys, in 1582 and 1623, which show that there were then some 15 or 16 dwellings, including the *George Inn*. A third survey, in 1776, describes some 27 dwellings, again including the

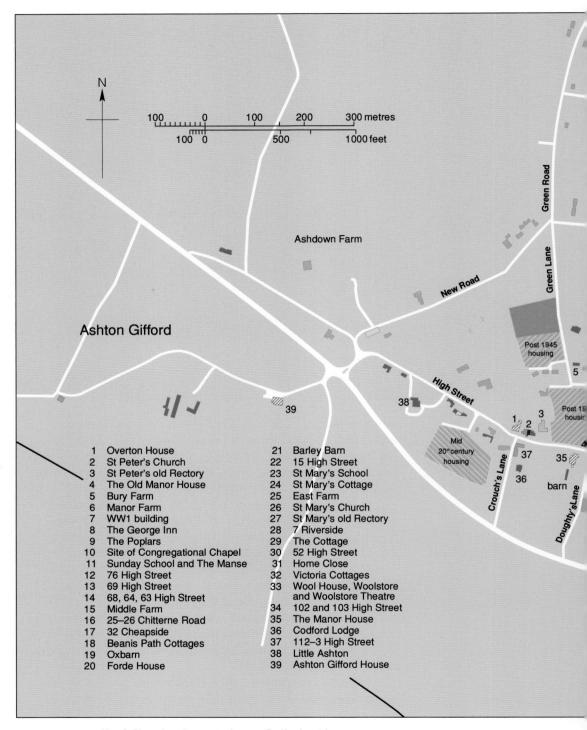

N

100 ___ 0 ___ 100 ___ 200 ___ 300 metres
100 ___ 0 ___ 500 ___ 1000 feet

Ashdown Farm

Green Road

Green Lane

New Road

Ashton Gifford

Post 1945
housing

High Street

39   38

Post 19
housir

1 3
2

Mid
20ᵗʰ century
housing

37   35

Crouch's Lane

36

barn

Doughty's Lane

1	Overton House	21	Barley Barn
2	St Peter's Church	22	15 High Street
3	St Peter's old Rectory	23	St Mary's School
4	The Old Manor House	24	St Mary's Cottage
5	Bury Farm	25	East Farm
6	Manor Farm	26	St Mary's Church
7	WW1 building	27	St Mary's old Rectory
8	The George Inn	28	7 Riverside
9	The Poplars	29	The Cottage
10	Site of Congregational Chapel	30	52 High Street
11	Sunday School and The Manse	31	Home Close
12	76 High Street	32	Victoria Cottages
13	69 High Street	33	Wool House, Woolstore and Woolstore Theatre
14	68, 64, 63 High Street	34	102 and 103 High Street
15	Middle Farm	35	The Manor House
16	25–26 Chitterne Road	36	Codford Lodge
17	32 Cheapside	37	112–3 High Street
18	Beanis Path Cottages	38	Little Ashton
19	Oxbarn	39	Ashton Gifford House
20	Forde House		

Map 8 Phased settlement in the two Codford parishes.

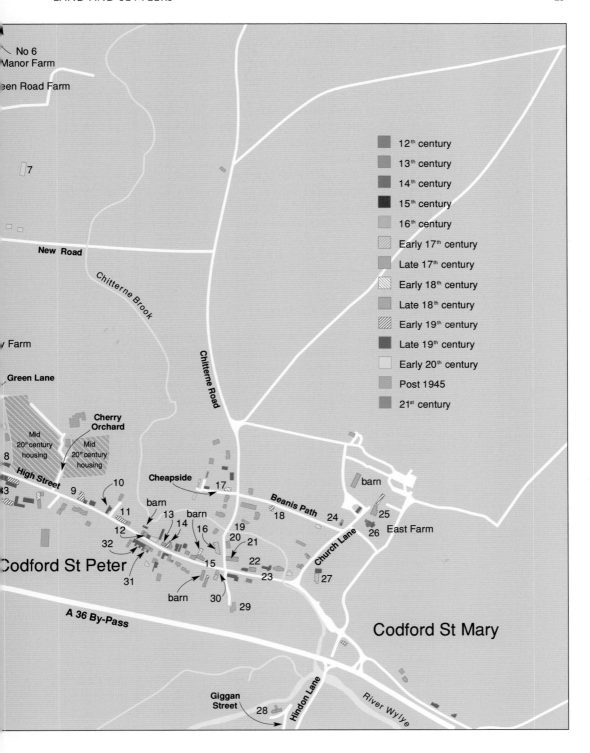

No 6
Manor Farm

een Road Farm

7

New Road

Chitterne Brook

Chitterne Road

Farm

Green Lane

Cherry
Orchard

Mid
20th century
housing

Mid
20th century
housing

High Street

Cheapside

barn

8

9

10

11

13

barn

14

barn

16

17

19

18

Beanis Path

24

barn

25

East Farm

26

Church Lane

20

21

12

32

15

22

23

27

Codford St Peter

31

barn

30

29

A 36 By-Pass

Codford St Mary

Giggan
Street

28

Hindon Lane

River Wylye

12th century
13th century
14th century
15th century
16th century
Early 17th century
Late 17th century
Early 18th century
Late 18th century
Early 19th century
Late 19th century
Early 20th century
Post 1945
21st century

inn. From maps and surviving buildings it is clear that ribbon development extended west of the church by *c.* 1700, and that by 1773 both sides of the main road were built up between the church and the *George* (see Map 8). Most of these buildings have now gone. Indeed from the 17th century only the core of the Old Rectory and the farmhouses known as Old Manor House and 112-13 High Street remain, 112-13 and the 18th-century French Horn reflecting the medieval pattern of properties lying end-on to the street (see Chapter 2).[18]

Ashton Gifford, set apart from the two Codfords in the south-west of the modern parish, was probably always smaller and unlike the others began to decline in the Middle Ages. A map of 1773 depicts only some nine buildings along what was then the road to Boyton and a lane leading eastwards from it. These houses survived until the building of Ashton Gifford House and the creation of its park in the early 19th century.

The Modern Village Emerges

The modern village of Codford has developed along the old main road from two, formerly separate, settlements that were focused around the medieval churches of St Mary and St Peter. Ashton Gifford, the third settlement, has remained an outsider, the bypass adding to its isolation. The maps in this book chart these developments.

The development of Codford was increasingly focused on the main road, which from the 18th century at least was of regional and perhaps national importance. Its significance was enhanced in 1761 when turnpike trusts were formed to improve it. Buildings grew or appeared in response to this, and some houses were given more eye-catching fronts. In Codford St Peter the *George Inn*, which served local and long-distance traffic, had a large stable courtyard in and probably before the mid-19th century when the Woolstore, opposite it, was built. No doubt the Woolstore was positioned on the road to take advantage of easy access for carts bringing wool from farms and taking it to the mills.[19]

At Codford St Mary, road improvement was accompanied by an increase in housing stock. The 35 inhabitable houses recorded between 1790 and 1811 had increased to 40 by 1821; although mostly along the main road, they included five at Malmpit, four in Cheapside, four in Giggan Street, and Stockton Lodge, guarding the entrance to Stockton Park by Hindon Lane. The rising population was reflected in further increases during the earlier 19th century, and the housing stock had risen to 92 by 1861. Some were replacements, others were on new sites at the western end of Cheapside

Figure 14 Stockton Lodge, the late 18th-century gate lodge to Stockton House, now separated from house and park by the Codford bypass.

and in Church Lane, but judging by map evidence and by what survives today many must have been formed by subdividing older houses (see Chapter 2).[20]

At Codford St Peter, intermittent eastward progress along the main road, especially on its north side, continued into the 19th century, and extended almost to the parish boundary with St Mary's, where the Congregational chapel was built in 1811 to serve the whole of Codford. By 1817, on the south side of the High Street there were more houses than there are now and they continued westward to Sherrington Lane, the site of an isolated building (gone by 1817) where it joined Crouch's Lane. Many of them were demolished in the 19th century.

By the early 19th century the number of inhabitable houses in Codford St Peter had risen to 56, more than double the number described in 1776. It increased further in the later 19th century, reaching 68 by 1891. New arrivals included a new farmstead called Bury Farm, a brewery building north of the *George Inn* (which was itself rebuilt in 1893), and Ivy Cottages on the main road west of the village. As in Codford St Mary, there were several replacements of older buildings, but here more of them took the form of detached residences, on the south side set back in their own large gardens (see Chapter 2).[21]

The development of Ashton Gifford, which lay apart from the main road, was strikingly different. When in the early 19th century Ashton Gifford House was built and its parkland laid out, most of the buildings on the former village site were demolished, and lanes and boundaries were altered or removed. In their place fishponds, withy beds, kennels, a coach house, two cottages and a granary were constructed.

While improvements and changes to the road pattern had a determining effect on the development of the three settlements, the railway had far less impact. Arriving in the 1850s, this former GWR branch line (now part of the Cardiff to Portsmouth route) required few major engineering works and passed through the parish almost unnoticed. It follows the line of the Wylye Valley south-west of Codford, crossing the river south of Codford St Peter and skirting the south-west corner of Ashton Gifford park road. Codford station, with the stationmaster's lodge nearby, opened in 1856 at the far south-west corner of the parish, and was linked to the main road by the realigned Boyton Lane, renamed Station Road.

As has already been noted, most building activity happened in or close to the nucleated centres of both parishes. The station remained isolated. The only effect of the coming of the railway was to engender the construction of a few buildings at Ashton Gifford.[22] The main reasons were probably the relative unimportance of the line (which linked Thingley Junction near Chippenham to Salisbury via Westbury), its location in the valley, and the difficulty in acquiring building land within the Ashton Gifford estate. In both main settlements, despite a rise in the population, fewer than three dozen houses were built or created out of others between the 1860s and 1914.[23]

The railway made its presence felt only with the onset of the First World War. Between 1914 and 1923, both it and the village changed dramatically and temporarily with the arrival of the army. Military branch lines were built by the War Office to link Codford Station with the Codford military camps and Codford and the other intermediate stations were provided with extra sidings and

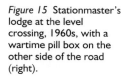

Figure 15 Stationmaster's lodge at the level crossing, 1960s, with a wartime pill box on the other side of the road (right).

loading bays (see Panel 15). The arrival of troops prompted a frenzy of new construction along the main road. Shops and cafés, temporary in appearance, sprung up in the front gardens of existing houses, and were joined by more conventional new building. By the time the camps closed in 1919, they contrived to fill almost all vacant plots in St Mary's parish along the north side of the main road, as well as blurring any remaining distinction between the two ancient parishes (see Chapter 7).[24]

Codford combined Thereafter, there was something of a lull in building activity. Such development as there was in the 1920s and 1930s was largely to the north of the main village and connected with New Road, to which a south-western extension, parallel to the closed line of the Codford camp railway, was added in 1924. To the north of that road, eight new council houses of 1937–8 marked the beginning of a new campaign of local authority house-building.

After 1945 the urgent need for housing prompted homeless families to take over 19 vacated army huts at Bury Camp, which they still occupied in 1951. By then, however, the local authority had begun to provide new housing much closer to the village centre, starting south of the High Street with the Grove, an estate of 22 houses, planned in 1948 round a small green. After 1952 another 20 houses built north of the main road on the site of the army huts began to knit together the two Codfords in a planned way. Between 1963 and 1975, 69 more houses were built in Cherry Orchard, to which a further 12 had been added by 1982. Despite the closure of Codford railway station in 1955, wider access to cars brought private housing developments at Oxbarn (off Chitterne Road) 1970-5; in Doughty Lane *c.*1989; at Broadleaze, 1993; and in Green Lane, begun 2002.[25]

Apart from new building, the most important changes to the character of the modern village have been linked with the main road, designated the Southampton to Bristol trunk road (A36). Motor traffic became a serious and growing problem. In the narrow section through Codford vehicles collided with walls and buildings, serious accidents occurred at minor road junctions, and the quality of life deteriorated. A road widening scheme was abandoned because it would have resulted in the loss of about 45 village buildings, although some piecemeal widening did occur during the 1960s and 1970s, and some buildings were wholly or partially demolished. A northern bypass taking a route by New Road and the Bury was suggested in 1946, and another in 1947, but neither was implemented. Meanwhile Cranborne Chase and the West Wiltshire Downs were designated an area of outstanding natural beauty in 1983, assuring Codford's unspoilt landscape setting.

Figure 16 The Wylye
Valley, showing the
railway passing through
it before the bypass was
built.

A public enquiry in 1987 resulted in the choice of a southern
route to bypass the village and preserve its immediate environs.
The new road, opened in 1990, meant realigning a short stretch
of the River Wylye and building an access road from the bypass
to the east end of the village. At the west end the northern end of
Sherrington Lane was used for access, and the old road was closed
off, leaving only one section of the old road at Malmpit Hill, east
of St Mary's church, open to serve the properties along it. Freed
from the threat of a bypass, development north of the village has
gathered pace and modern maps reveal a scatter of late 20th-
century housing on previously occupied sites, while infill such as
Quinton Close off The Bury has increased the density of buildings
in the heart of the village.[26]

Population

Before the Census It is difficult to work put how many people lived
in these settlements before the population censuses of the 19th
century began to provide precise figures. Estimates have generally
to be based on calculations derived from numbers of household-
ers, taxpayers or churchgoers. The earliest assessment possible
derives from Domesday Book, 1086, which records 16 households
in Codford St Mary, 12 in St Peter, and 10 in Ashton Gifford. If an
average household included four individuals this would translate to
a total population of 152, with 64 living in St Mary, 48 in St Peter
and 40 in Ashton Gifford. But such calculations cannot be trusted,
since the size of an 11th-century household is unknowable.[27]

At national level population rose significantly to *c.*1300 and then
fell. In Codford a tax assessment of 1332 recorded 16 households in
Ashton Gifford and 60 in the combined Codfords, precisely double
the total in 1086. Poor families were exempt, however, and others

who should have paid may have evaded the tax; no accurate population figure is possible, therefore, although the total is unlikely to have been less than 300 to 400. More precise was the first poll tax, levied in 1377 on everyone over 14 years old. Codford returned 171 and Ashton Gifford 28, so with children added the total parish population may have approached 300, almost certainly a decline. More significant is the relative dwindling of Ashton Gifford, from 26 per cent of parish households in 1086, to 21 per cent in 1332 and 14 per cent of adults in 1377.[28]

Three centuries separate the 1377 poll tax from the next significant headcount, a census of communicants and dissenters taken in 1676. This recorded 130 communicants in St Peter's parish and 89 in St Mary's, with one Catholic dissenter, 220 altogether. If this is taken as the adult population, the total population probably lay between 300 and 400 once again, with St Peter's considerably more populous than St Mary's.[29] No hearth tax returns survive against which we might test these estimates for accuracy.

The Census Reliable total population figures have been provided by a census taken every ten years since 1801 (except 1941). From 1951 the two Codfords have been enumerated as one, but all previous censuses recorded St Mary and St Peter separately. From the table and graph clear trends emerge (see Panel 2). As elsewhere in rural Wiltshire, Codford's combined population trended upwards until the mid-19th century and then declined, from around 500 in 1811 to nearly 800 in 1851 and back to a little over 500 in 1901. The universal drift from country to town explains much of the downturn, exacerbated in Codford's case not just by agricultural depression, but also by the closure of the wool-stapling business and the racing stables. After 1901 Codford's population remained little more than 500 until the mid-20th century and then, as new local authority and private housing became available, stabilised around 700, but rising above 800 in 2001. Except in 1921, when a few military personnel remained to inflate the total, the census figures mask the enormous temporary influxes of people Codford had to accommodate during the two world wars.[30]

Within Codford the fortunes of St Mary's and St Peter's parishes have differed. In 1801 St Peter's (with Ashton Gifford) was twice as populous as St Mary's, but progressively St Mary's took a larger share, so that by 1861 it had overtaken St Peter's. It continued the larger partner until 1901, but thereafter until the two amalgamated in 1934 their populations were almost the same.

Census Returns

Like many statistical sources, the totals provided by the national censuses made every decade since 1841 can supply the historian with invaluable information but can also be misleading. The Codford totals were given separately for St Mary and St Peter until 1931, when they disappeared as administrative units. In 1841 Ashton Gifford and Codford St Peter were also distinguished. The graph shows clearly the upward trend of population until the 1850s and then a steady decline, characteristic of rural communities during the later 19th century. It also reveals the shifting balance of the two Codford parishes, St Mary's growing faster to mid-century, St Peter's declining faster thereafter. What it does not show, because no totals were taken between 1911 and 1921 or between 1931 and 1951, is the enormous influx of service personnel during the two world wars, overwhelming the local population.

Totals such as these, useful or misleading, are only a small fraction of the information that the national censuses offer historians. The returns upon which from 1841 to 1901 the Victorian censuses were based are particularly important and are open for inspection. For every member of the population they record name and approximate address, family relationships, age, occupation,

A page of the 1881 Codford St Mary census return.

disabilities, and parish of origin. They are a most valuable resource for researching social history within the context of a single community or for tracing an individual's family history.

Copies of census returns are available at local record offices and/or local studies libraries. Some census information is freely available online, and much more can be searched on a subscription basis. Local statistical information derived from censuses is summarised on the Vision of Britain website www.visionofbritain.org.uk, and for Wiltshire, 1801–1951 parish totals are given in *VCH Wilts* 4, 315-61.

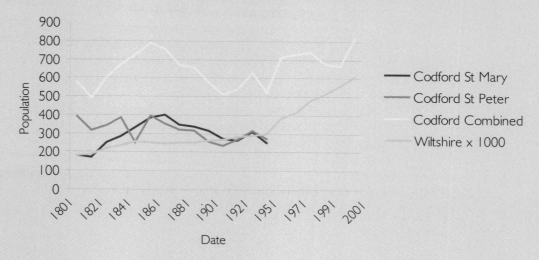

Codford Population Totals 1801–2001

Chapter 2

Building the Village

Travellers who leave the A36 in favour of the old Warminster to Salisbury road experience Codford, not as three separate settlements that have grown together, but as one village most of which spreads along the High Street. A closer look reveals that the oldest houses are clustered close to the parish churches, the ancient centres of the two Codfords. More recent ones lie not only on the fringes but in the centre of the modern village, having been built on open ground between two of the original settlements. The unplanned character of the village with its haphazard mix of buildings may have developed because Codford's lords of the manor were rarely resident and had little interest in providing standard farmhouses, consistent cottage rows and public amenities. Some of the earliest houses were built as farmhouses or farm buildings and their gardens were farmyards that opened onto the village street and, on its south side, on to closes of land behind. In the 19th century villas, new farmhouses and the stark new Woolstore appeared and it was not until the 20th century that planned additions were made to the village in the shape of council housing and small speculative developments. In contrast, at Ashton

Figure 17 St Mary's Cottage has been adapted gradually, using easily available building materials. Like many similar small houses, it had a living room, in which cooking was done, and a parlour. Both rooms were heated from a central chimneystack.

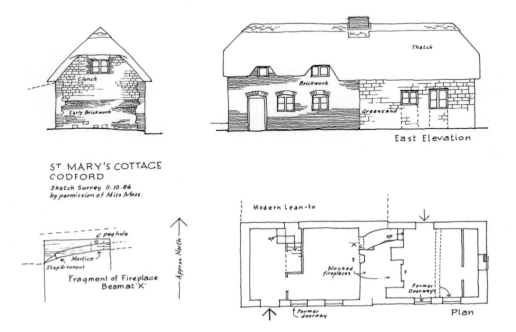

Thatch

Clunch

Early Brickwork

Brickwork

Greensand

East Elevation

ST MARY'S COTTAGE
CODFORD
*Sketch Survey 11·10·86
by permission of Miss Moss.*

peghole

Mortice
Step & runout

Fragment of Fireplace
Beam at 'X'

Approx. North

Modern Lean-to

up   up
F
X
blocked
fireplaces   F
Former
Doorways

Former
doorway   Plan

Gifford there are no old farmhouses. There a single landowner, having acquired a large parcel of land in the 19th century, swept away the ancient settlement to create a parkland landscape round a new country house.[31]

Codford's buildings are typical in materials and style of this part of Wiltshire. Until the mid 19th century all but the wealthiest inhabitants used a mixture of locally found materials, such as clay to make cob and later brick, timber, limestone rubble, blocks of chalk, and flint. Good stone was expensive to transport. It was only imported for the most prestigious work, such as the sculptured stone in St Peter's church for which high quality Bath stone was brought in the 9th century from as far away as north Wiltshire. Even when transport improved in the 19th century, dressed stone was usually restricted to details on brick buildings.[32]

CHURCHES AND CHAPEL

Figure 18 St Mary's church from the southwest. Its prominent Victorian aisle hides the genuinely medieval nave and chancel in this view.

Codford's buildings document changes in social status, working life and religious practice, supplementing the written and mapped record. Most remarkable and oldest are the two parish churches, which predate any other building in Codford by some 400 years. Both lie at the foot of the downs, slightly raised above the river

Figure 19 St Peter's church, which stood at the entrance to the medieval village from the west, was made more impressive in the 15th century by battlemented additions.

Wylye, on sites established when the Anglo-Saxon churches of Codford St Mary and Codford St Peter were founded. St Peter's may have replaced a substantial Anglo-Saxon church, for which the Codford Cross was perhaps carved about AD 800 to decorate the building (see Panel 3).

The churches were rebuilt in the 12th century, St Mary's probably at least 30 years before St Peter's. Both were built of limestone at a time when other village buildings must have been of timber or earth-walled. What they might have looked like then can be judged only from the fragments that survive inside the buildings and from paintings made before restoration work in the 19th century. Although each long rectangular church seems to have had no more than a nave and a chancel, neither was entirely plain. St Mary's, which was begun before 1150, still has its early 12th-century chancel arch, decorated to mark the division between the public space of the nave and the sacred area in which Mass was celebrated. The arch is visible from the chancel but has been hidden from the nave by a second arch, built on its west side about 50 years later. The earlier arch is round and unmoulded and supported by shafts with capitals in the form of cushions. The north capital is carved with grapes in reference to the wine used in the Mass and the south one with scrolls, known as volutes. Two fragments lying loose in the church may also have been capitals from the chancel arch and one of them is decorated with a pattern of interwoven strands (interlace), which continues the tradition seen on the Codford Stone.

The later, west-facing arch, and perhaps some loose stones carved with chevron ornament and beasts' heads, probably formed part of a scheme to modernise the whole church. The builders

Figure 20 The chancel arch in St Peter's, drawn *c.*1804 by the antiquary John Buckler, who recorded many churches before they were altered by the Victorians. The arch was similar in style to early fabric at St Mary's.

Figure 21 St Peter's church was enlarged in the 15th century, when the south porch was added. The approach to it was improved in the 19th century after the road level was lowered, probably because of turnpiking.

of the west arch chose a style midway between that of the first, Romanesque arch and the Gothic used when most of the church was rebuilt in the 13th and 14th centuries. They gave the arch a pointed and moulded head, capitals with stylized leaves (waterleaf), moulded shaft rings and bases with deep grooves, aptly described as waterholding.

Each church has a font, which is one of the most important and long-lasting of liturgical items in any church. Each was carved in the 12th century from a single piece of stone and, although it seems likely that they were made for these buildings, there can be no certain proof without documents, pictures or physical evidence. Many loose items of furnishing and decoration find homes distant from their original destinations. [33]

The rector of each parish was responsible for maintaining the chancel of his church. About 1200 the rectors of St Mary's and St Peter's made fashionable eastward extensions to the chancels, thereby distancing the high altar from the congregation and enhancing the mystery of the Mass. St Peter's chancel was given a group of three stepped seats (sedilia), which suggests that more than one priest served the church at that time. The ornate character of the sedilia and fragments of stained glass and of a tomb effigy at St Mary's indicate that, although their architecture may have been quite plain, the churches were richly decorated. We get an impression of St Mary's medieval appearance from the antiquary Revd James Ingram, who recorded many features uncovered during rebuilding work in 1843–4. He noted traces of dark red fresco painting and a running scrollwork pattern, as well as remains of a holy water stoup (basin) and of a rood screen which had closed off the chancel from nave and restricted the congregation's view of the Mass to what was possible through a squint opening.[34]

Parishioners looked after the upkeep of naves and towers which, in both Codfords, received a great deal of attention after 1300. At St Mary's a new nave was built and given traceried windows of two lights and, in the second half of the 14th century, a new tower and south porch were added to it. Major landowners and entrepreneurs with local connections were often the main contributors to new work; for example, at St Peter's the Hungerfords probably paid for building the south porch after 1485, when they regained their Codford property, and it was probably also during that period that the nave was rebuilt and the south side of the church became a show front to the main road.[35]

After the Reformation

Both churches must have been considerably altered to fit the new forms of worship instituted after the Reformation. It was surely then that the squint and holy water stoup were walled up at St Mary's, the rood loft was removed and the colourfully painted walls whitewashed. Baptism and preaching were important parts of the reformed liturgy and a 17th-century pyramidal font cover survives at St Peter's and a richly carved pulpit at St Mary's, where John Mompesson was rector from 1612 until 1646. The Mompesson family made clear their importance in the parish by erecting the handsome monument that is now in the south chapel. Its accurate classical details and finely executed carving resemble those on the Salisbury cathedral tomb of Sir Richard Mompesson (died 1627). The Codford tomb probably commemorated the lord of the manor, Richard Mompesson who died in 1584, although it may not have been installed until Richard's relative, John, repaired the chancel in 1622. The tomb probably stood in the chancel, a prominent position to which the family were entitled as lords of the manor and owners of the rectory estate (see Chapter 6). The fragmentary effigies that lie on it probably belonged to other dismantled monuments.[36]

We know from records that by 1783 the church furnishings in St Mary's were very simple – there was a communion table and a reading desk, both covered with cloths, and a parish chest – and that no bequests had been made for the upkeep of the nave, for which the parishioners remained responsible. In 1807 when the chancel was repaired again, according to the incised stones on the east wall, the rest of the church was probably in poor repair.[37]

Figure 22 St Peter's medieval roof was replaced by a very low-pitched one, invisible in Buckler's drawing of *c.*1804. The roof and other features, such as post-medieval chancel windows and the top of the tower, have been altered by the Victorians.

The Anglo-Saxon Sculptured Stone

Discovered built into the wall above the chancel arch of St Peter's in 1864, the Anglo-Saxon sculpture now stands against the north chancel wall. A single, tapering block of Bath stone from the Chalfield area (north Wiltshire), 1.25m high and split lengthwise, it was probably carved on all its faces; one broad face was lost when the stone was split. The carving is deep-cut and the detail well-preserved. It is likely that the unweathered stone has always been within a church on the site of the present St Peter's.

The main face depicts a man in a short tunic and cloak, wearing a headband. He is in a strange posture – half turned with his right leg raised and the foot pointing groundwards. His head is thrown back, his right hand lifted up to grasp the stem of a fruiting plant and his left at his side, holding a globular implement or vessel with a long handle or stem. The two narrow faces display plant-scrolls, a form of decoration derived from Mediterranean or Near-Eastern ornament featuring vines. They allude to Christ, who in a famous passage in St John's Gospel (15, 1-10) described himself as the True Vine.

The sculpture has been the subject of much speculation. First, when was it made? Anglo-Saxon sculpture rarely bears dates or inscriptions and the Codford stone is no exception. It has to be dated by assessing the style of carving and the subject matter in comparison with other material – including manuscript illumination, metalwork, and ivory carving. On this basis, the stone is generally ascribed to the late eighth or early ninth century.

To what kind of feature did it belong? The fact that it tapers has led to the belief that it formed part or all of the main shaft of a cross. The cult of the Cross on which Christ was crucified goes back to early Christian times and found expression in Anglo-Saxon England in the erection of free-standing stone monuments with tall rectangular or round shafts surmounted by a cross-shaped head and often adorned with sculpture. Such crosses could be in the open air or (as in the case of Codford) could form part of the internal decoration of a church. Possibly, however, the sculpture was not part of a cross at all, but formed an element in some internal architectural feature, perhaps flanking an opening. But whatever its purpose, the church to which it belonged is likely to have been a grand and richly decorated building.

Figure A: *The broad face of the Codford stone.*

Figure B: *A sculptured stone originally from Sheffield and now in the British Museum. Virtually contemporary with that from Codford, it depicts an archer in a similar short tunic entangled in a vine scroll.*

Last of all, who is depicted and what is he doing? This has been much debated, partly because there are few if any real parallels. Although the figure's posture has been compared with that of an archer preparing to draw his bow (Fig. B), he clearly has no such weapon. A closer parallel is the boy harvesting grapes on a late ninth-century metal strap end recently found in Cranborne (Dorset) (Fig. C). This scene has been interpreted as a reference to the wine of the Eucharist, even perhaps to Christ, the True Vine in whom the faithful dwell (John 15, 1-4). Perhaps the Codford figure is a similar symbolic harvester, holding aloft a fruiting vine in one hand and clutching a wine-flask in the other.

Or perhaps the figure is a dancer, in fact the Biblical King David, triumphant over the Philistines. Before the battle, David had been instructed by the Lord to wait among fruit trees until the rustling of their leaves should provide the signal to attack, while after the victory he had danced unrestrainedly with harps and cymbals before the Ark (2 Samuel, 5-6). The fruiting tree could commemorate the grove where David waited, while the figure is the king himself, wearing not a headband but a royal diadem and holding not a flask but a musical instrument. Regarded as the ancestor of Christ and author of the Old Testament book of Psalms, David was a key figure for the Anglo-Saxons, often depicted, though no comparable scene showing him dancing is known.

Although its meaning and function will continue to be discussed, Codford's Anglo-Saxon sculpture is a celebrated and distinguished work of art; it remains proof of the skill, taste and creativity of those associated with Codford more than twelve hundred years ago.

For sources see Bibliography.

Alan Thacker

Figure C: *A strap end found near Cranborne showing a youth in a short tunic holding a knife and climbing through a vine.*

Figure 23 The architect, T.H. Wyatt, depicted himself in St Mary's instructing the mason in the execution of his ideal design. He also shows the nave clear of seating, the chancel of later accretions, and the Mompesson tomb in his new south chapel.

Figure 24 The plan of St Mary's, showing the proposed improvements in red, shows that the church was almost doubled in size in the 1840s.

Victorian Transformation

Victorian restorations transformed both churches into an idealised approximation of their medieval selves, to which the gradual accretion of donated furnishings and fittings added a High Anglican richness and complexity. They were designed by the London architect T.H. Wyatt, who was employed as Salisbury Diocesan architect and who has gained a reputation for cavalier rearrangement of original fabric. At St Mary's enlargement and installation of a gallery had already been considered in 1836, but it was only following the collapse of the south wall near the chancel that work began in 1843–4. Wyatt (in partnership with David Brandon) added a south aisle and south-eastern chapel with organ chamber in Decorated Gothic style. The south porch was also rebuilt in a new position, the buttressing of the north nave wall was strengthened, the west door restyled, and part of the chancel was taken down and rebuilt with a renewed window. James Ingram, who recorded the medieval features then obliterated and who had died in 1850, was commemorated with a late Gothic style wall monument above the south door.[38]

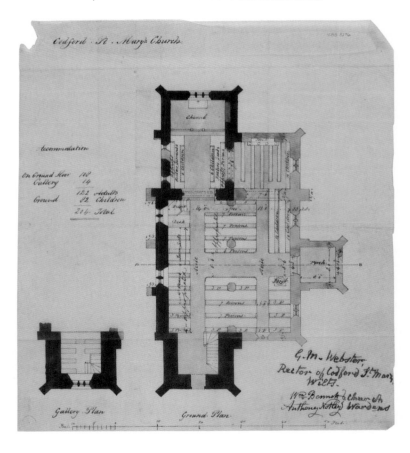

In 1863–5, 20 years after he had worked at St Mary's, T.H. Wyatt restored, reseated, and enlarged St Peter's church with a character-istically heavy hand and, in the chancel, new north aisle, and north organ chamber, a pervasive 13th-century Gothic style. Nave and chancel were reroofed at a steeper pitch considered appropriate to the chosen style, and the chancel was enriched with naturalistic carving, stained glass, and encaustic tiles. The porch was almost entirely reconstructed internally with an elaborate vault and the work was, unusually, dedicated to a woman by a woman friend – to Sophia Ravenhill (died 1863) by Maria Waldron, who had paid for it. In contrast, the new aisle and organ chamber, hidden from the road on the north side, were much plainer and look utilitarian.[39]

Despite all the work done in 1843–4, by 1878 St Mary's church was described as dark, damp and in general decay, and needed to be reseated, refloored, and repaired. The external appearance was mainly unaffected, but a vestry was added, and the arcade piers were rebuilt in circular form by E.H. Lingen Barker of Hereford. Of the many monuments repositioned then most important was the Mompesson tomb which, as Wyatt had planned in the earlier restoration, was moved to the south wall of the south chapel. The last major structural work in the 19th century was the underpin-ning of St Peter's tower in 1898. That church was significantly repaired in 1972–3, with a lighter touch than that employed by Wyatt, and by 2002 the congregation's desire for a space for more informal events had been accommodated by removing the pews from the north aisle.[40]

The Congregationalists

Figure 25 The Congregational chapel, its school and manse were originally ranged along the street. The chapel's large upper windows lit a gallery inside.

The plain brick chapel and single-storeyed schoolroom that the Congregationalists built in 1811 had no architectural ambition beyond the slightly Gothic windows in the schoolroom. The neighbouring manse, however, has an elegant stuccoed front with sash windows and classical doorcase and may have been built as the congregation swelled towards the mid-19th century, when the chapel itself was enlarged or rebuilt. The chapel remained a plain building, with tall gallery windows, which, as congregations dwin-dled in the 20th century, fell into dereliction and was demolished. Schoolroom and manse have been converted into private houses.

HOUSES AND FARMS

Nothing remains of the medieval houses of Codford nor of the
cottages built for the poorest. In contrast, over a dozen stone and
timber-framed houses, almost equally distributed between the
parishes, reveal that a considerable amount of building was going
on between about 1580 and 1700. In Codford St Peter alone, of
approximately nineteen houses recorded in 1776, nine remain,
of which five had been built before 1700. Most of Codford's early
houses have been changed out of immediate recognition or exist
only as fragments. For example, the Oxbarn, which stands on the
east side of the Chitterne Road on the site of the former ox yard,
was apparently built as a late 16th-century single-celled, timber-
framed cottage but has been almost engulfed in 18th- and 20th-
century alterations.

Most houses lie along the main road and were built by families
who owned or rented small plots of land. Their accommodation
was restricted to a hall – an everyday living room – and parlour,
which were usually entered from a cross-passage between the
two rooms, and to garrets above for storage and sleeping. At least
three houses remain that were built for people of higher status
and greater wealth. The grandest is the rectory house at Codford
St Peter, which had been built shortly before 1608. Of the three
more lavish houses only this one had private bedchambers in a
full-height upper storey. It also had a dedicated entrance through
a lobby in front of the central chimney stack, an arrangement
known as a lobby-entry. Though the highest status house in
Codford St Mary, the rectory house, was built about the same time
– probably during the incumbency of John Mompesson – it had
a less sophisticated plan, with a hall, parlour, and a cross-passage

Map 9 The surviving
buildings that date
from the 16th and 17th
centuries.

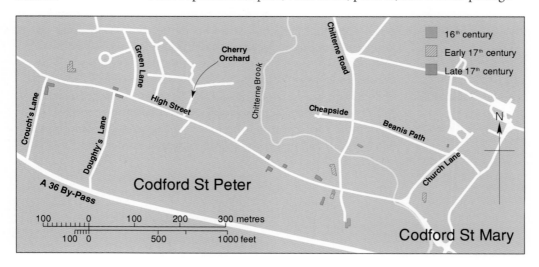

Figure 26 The Old Manor House, typical of stone-built West Wiltshire farmhouses of the late 16th and early 17th centuries. A front door, now blocked, led into the everyday living room (hall). The central chimneystack was used to heat both hall and the parlour, which was slightly raised above a cellar (right). Note signs of a change in the road level and windows divided into lights by vertical members (mullions).

running behind the central chimney stack. In plan and elevation, and with its limestone and thatch construction, that rectory house must have resembled the so-called Old Manor House at Codford St Peter, the most complete of Codford's 17th-century stone houses partly due to a mid-20th-century restoration. Its superior external finish, the inclusion of a cellar under the parlour, and former lavish internal features, such as panelling, decorative plasterwork and a classically carved fireplace, indicate that the occupants of the Old Manor House were distinctly more affluent than Codford's other farmers. They may have been responsible for the manor's home farm, which probably lay in this part of the village. After about 1650 other new houses went up on the north side of the main road in Codford St Mary. They include the present 69 and 76 High Street, and Middle Farm, which was by far the largest house and, although they are related in style to the Old Manor House, each was built with two full storeys and end chimney stacks, one of which supported the stair.[41]

Most of the houses built before 1650 seem to have been constructed with large-panelled timber frames; the use of limestone rubble was restricted to the section of the hall that contained the fire (the fire bay), to plinths and to gable walls. Such construction was used for both for the high status rectory house at Codford St Peter and for small farmhouses, such as 52 High Street, which lies end-on to the street in Codford St Mary. Some houses probably had timber fire bays when first built. The Cottage had a stone one from the beginning, but the stone chimney stack was not added to the one-and-a-half-storeyed late 16th-century 52 until the house was reconstructed in the 17th century. Stone gable ends can be seen at the two-storeyed 25–6 Chitterne Road, and a similar house is incorporated in Codford St Peter at 102 High Street. Cob, which

Figure 27 Nos 52-4 is one of the small farmhouses built end-on to the south side of High Street, siting that gave easy access to each farmer's close of land. The timber-framing is functional rather than decorative and alterations, such as division into two houses, numerous.

is clay mixed with straw, was a common, immediately available building material. It was probably widely used, although little can be identified now. It has been found as garden walls, particularly of the rectory houses, at the isolated one-and-a-half-storeyed lobby-entry Ashton Cottage in Station Road, and at Home Close (formerly Shirley House), where it was used to build the front and rear ground-floor walls of the west end of the house; the second storey of stone was added later. The thick rendered walls of other houses might also encase cob construction. [42]

Modernisation and New Building 1700–1800

After 1700 fewer new houses were built but many were enlarged. The materials used for new buildings were even more varied than in the previous century, although thatch remained usual for roofing. An interest in decorative effect can be seen in depictions of two lost buildings, one an outwardly 18th-century cottage which stood on the site of Forde House in Chitterne Road until 1902, the other the 18th-century stone Gardener's Cottage, which until 1964 stood in the grounds of the Manor House. They both had long straw thatch decoratively sewn round the edges, a type of thatching that seems to have fallen from use in the area. Comparable effects were used in walling, for example by creating chequer patterns with flint and chalk, as for example at 2 French Horn, and in contrasts of brick and stone. Brick made its first appearance as prestigious facing at the four-bayed 103 High Street, with limestone used for the rest. Limestone was also used for the gable ends, if not more, at Overton House, but the remodelling of 112–13 High Street, almost opposite, was done in greensand blocks, probably in 1722 if the inscribed plaque can be believed. Greensand was also used for the barn attached to Middle Farm, Codford St Mary, perhaps in about 1712. The former Barley Barn, which in 1840 was owned by the rector of Codford St Mary and stands on the north side of the High Street, just beyond the junction with Chitterne Road, was built partly with stone and partly with timber believed to have come from Deptford (near Wylye) – a rare case where the source of timber can perhaps be identified.[43]

Domestic improvements Most domestic improvements were designed to fulfil the growing desire among well-established households for greater privacy and for living spaces free of most services. Additional private chambers, usually bedrooms, were created by building an extra storey or by creating lighted rooms within the roof space. This was done at the Old Manor House,

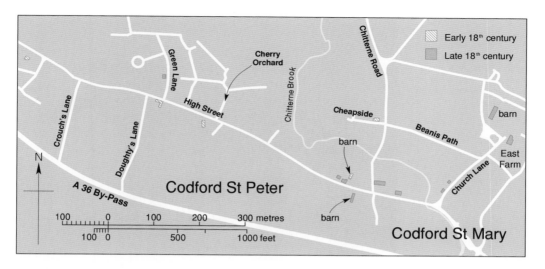

Map 10 The surviving buildings that were newly built or much altered in the 18th century.

Figure 28 The French Horn, showing the use of local materials. The roof is thatched and chalk blocks combined with flint make a patterned façade.

where upper rooms were made by raising sections of the walls in brick, and by inserting wooden casements windows and a new staircase. Two-storeyed extensions, containing a parlour or kitchen and chambers, were often added to the ends of two-room houses, a change that occurred at both rectory houses. Probably soon after 1705, a parlour and chambers were added to the east end of Codford St Mary's rectory and the original house was raised by a whole timber-framed storey. A hipped roof was constructed over the length of the house, and was probably covered from the outset not in thatch but in the clay tiles recorded in 1783. At Codford St Peter, the old rectory was modernized and a brick kitchen and chamber extension added on the north. Although the work at Codford St Peter was probably done only a decade or so later than that at Codford St Mary, its more elaborate chimney pieces and staircase, and timber sashes rather than mullioned windows, gave the house a far more sophisticated and classical appearance.[44]

Less ambitious improvements made to the smaller properties can be spotted throughout the village. In Codford St Mary, for example, 52 High Street was raised with eyebrow dormers and lengthened twice in brick (now a row including 53 and 54), while stone parlour bays were added to The Cottage and to Home Close, and a similar one was added to 102 High Street in Codford St Peter. Other detached houses were extended to form pairs of dwellings. At Codford St Peter an L-plan 17th-century house, 112–13 High Street, was made into a pair with an almost symmetrical front, probably about 1722; and at Codford St Mary a tiny 17th-century one-room house, 7 Riverside in Giggan Street, was raised, and the flint and brick at 8 added to it. The process of expansion continued

Figure 29 The rectory house of Codford St Mary. Its two-storey, hipped roofed form resulted from alterations made early in the 18th century when new rooms were added.

Figure 30 The rectory house of Codford St Peter. Its classical front conceals a 17th-century house, with a central chimney and lobby-entry plan.

into the 19th century when the 18th-century St Mary's Cottage, Church Lane, of clunch and brick, was similarly extended using greensand.[45]

Village Growth 1800–1914

Codford had no country seat until the early 19th century when Ashton Gifford House, set in a small ornamental park, took that role. Its peculiar plan and ungainly neoclassical appearance seem to have been the result of the incomplete house passing from owner to owner over quite a short period. Benjamin Rebbeck, who

Figure 31 Ashton Gifford House has a grand entrance hall converted from earlier reception rooms. Its staircase, with swept mahogany handrail and stick balusters, is typical of the earlier 19th century.

bought the property in 1806, seems to have begun the house. He was probably responsible for its two and a half storeyed centre, which at the front is three windows wide and has a Tuscan portico, but at the back has only two widely-spaced windows on each floor. He may have left the house as a shell when he lost his estate to his mortgagor, William Hubbard, who probably added the outer ashlar-faced bays between 1815 and 1824. These east and west additions gave the new owner four large reception rooms, with bedrooms above, in two tall storeys. To make a more impressive approach to the new rooms he filled the centre of the house with a staircase hall and saloon. It may have been Wadham Locke, the owner from 1836 to1850, who gave the ground-floor rooms their pretty early Victorian decoration.[46]

Growing together The two distinct settlements began to draw together as houses were built between them, and by 1886 they had almost joined up. From the surviving evidence it seems that although more building projects were undertaken in St Mary's parish, St Peter's had the grandest new private houses. Most of the early 19th-century houses – the remodelled Overton House, the Poplars, the Old Manse – were built on the north side of High Street. At least three new houses in Codford St Peter took the

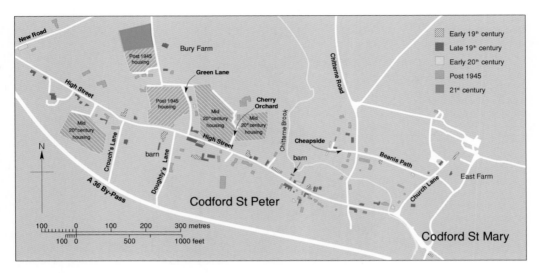

Map 11 How the village grew from the 19th century because of new building and alterations to old houses.

form of simple classical three-bayed, two-storeyed villas facing the street from behind small gardens with cast-iron railings. All had simple plans arranged round a central staircase hall. Overton House was built almost entirely of red brick with stone quoins on the site of Hungerford House, which is mentioned in the 1776 manorial survey as being close to St Peter's church, and it seems to retain the cellar of the older house. It was almost certainly built for the Codford surgeon, Isaac Flower, and his family, residents wealthy enough to have needed the separate service wing, and a gig house converted from a cob and stone outhouse. Other houses were given fashionable classical features, such as the tripartite sash windows used on the east front of Codford St Mary rectory house and at Middle Farm, which was transformed into a fashionable villa with a pilastered entrance to a central staircase hall and railed front garden.[47]

Figure 32 Overton House, seen from its garden. The main block, containing the reception rooms, is well-finished with stone angle quoins and a hipped slate roof. The service accommodation is much plainer.

Figure 33 Cottages in Doughty Lane. These one-up, one-down 18th-century cottages stood until the 1990s and were late survivals of the type of buildings once to be found in the lanes leading south from High Street.

One completely new house, very tall and impressive, Gothic in style and faced in expensive Bath stone, was Codford Lodge. It was built in 1862 close to the rectory in the grounds of Stable Cottage (112 High Street) by Charles Whitewick, then rector of Codford St Peter, for his four daughters. Two or three of the new houses in Codford St Mary were much more modestly built of rubble and brick: 63 High Street was one-up, one-down, and 64 was two-up, two-down; each had its kitchen or scullery in a lean-to extension (an outshut). Both houses have been demolished, but their character can be judged from 68 High Street, a similar though slightly later house. Even smaller one-up, one-down cottages survived in a row of four in Doughty Lane until the mid-1990s. The oldest of these was built in stone and flint chequer-pattern, with a brick extension above and may have been a late 18th-century cottage, heightened and extended into a row in the 19th century.[48]

Villagers continued to enlarge their homes, giving them extra rooms with distinct purposes. Both rectory houses had been extended again by 1886. Improvements of the kind that had, by 1783, provided Codford St Mary's rectory house with a large hall, parlour, kitchen, scullery, four bedrooms, and four garrets, were not made at Codford St Peter's rectory for about another 50 years. Then the house was extended west in brick to accommodate drawing room, dining room and bedrooms; a study was partitioned from the entrance hall within the 17th-century part; and the service range was extended again. At Codford St Mary's rectory house too, services were improved when an unadorned two-storeyed stone block with plain mullioned windows was built on the north side. Other village houses were enlarged in a less pretentious though socially significant way. For example, at Home Close (once the Post Office and for a time Shirley House), a half

Figure 34 Starveall Farm was built in the 19th century by Harry Biggs, a landowner who could afford to build both new farmhouse and farm buildings in red brick to an ordered plan.

Figure 35 Beanis
Path perhaps once an
important route from
Codford St Mary's
church. By the First
World War the only old
houses were this pair
of cottages (in the left
background behind the
army huts), designed
in traditional style
apparently for estate
workers.

storey and a south-west wing were added to the mid-17th-century
thatched cottage, possibly after 1847 when James Roxbee bought
the house.

Farms away from High Street were improved or newly built.
East Farm was much reconstructed and both Manor Farm, built on
farmland some distance north of Codford St Peter, and Bury Farm,
on its northern outskirts, included plain classical houses in a style
then thought fit for a gentleman. New brick and weather-boarded
farm buildings were erected at all three farms, those at Manor
Farm around three sides of a farmyard enclosed on the fourth by
cast-iron railings. Among the Biggs's improvements was the downland farmstead built at Starveall by Harry Biggs, which has become
a rare survival of a mid-19th-century type into the 21st century.[49]

A pair of cottages was built in the early 19th century, end-on
to Beanis Path, which runs between the Chitterne Road and
Church Lane. They were no doubt built as farmworkers' cottages,
and are a good example of their type, little altered over the years,
of coursed chalk block and with a hipped thatched roof with an
axial brick stack. They are single-storeyed with an attic each and
eyebrow dormers.[50]

The Changing High Street The character of High Street, particularly
in Codford St Peter, changed dramatically in the middle of the
19th century, when large new buildings appeared on the south side.
The complex of the Woolstore, Wool House, and Wool Cottage
(described in detail below) must have seemed an uncompromising
industrial intrusion into the otherwise rural street. On open ground
west of the Woolstore were built two large ashlar-faced houses
designed to face west. The first of these is the heavily classical

Figure 36 Manor Farm. The house shows how a gentleman farmer chose to live in the 19th century. The elegant façade is conservative with features, such as the classical doorcase and tripartite windows, that had long been popular.

Manor House, probably the successor to the main house on the manor of Codford St Peter. This house had been commandeered since at least the early 17th century as the manorial steward's temporary abode and livery when he and his retinue came, periodically, to collect rents. The building can be followed through the manorial records and surveys to 1812, when the manor of Codford St Peter was sold. There is substantial cellarage beneath the house and the kitchen area is probably the core of the old messuage. Further west is Ashton Villa (later Little Ashton), built between 1850 and 1861, possibly by Herbert Swayne Ingram; with its high basement storey and Franco-Flemish style, it looks incongruously urban. Soon after, around 1865, an equally urban-looking terrace of gabled stone houses, Victoria Cottages, was attached to Home Close, then the Post Office, by the Ford family, who were builders living there.[51]

In the later 19th century and earlier 20th several of the smarter High Street houses were altered. A balustraded porch was added to Overton House around 1889, as was a room over the porch at The Poplars, which was also extended about 1873–4 by a single-storeyed wing with its own street entrance that was originally a tailor's shop, but in about 1889 became a surgery for the local doctor, George Frederick Chadwick. The Manor House was also remodelled, especially inside, and Little Ashton was extended slightly in 1907. Codford St Peter's rectory house too was slightly improved in 1885. After 1850 the villas and farmhouses in the High Street were joined by smaller brick cottages and, in 1875–6, the picturesquely composed Codford St Mary Church of England school, which was enlarged in 1889–91.[52]

In 1893 the ancient *George Inn*, which had stood on the site since at least the late 16th century, was replaced by a smaller hotel,

Figure 37 The Poplars, built in the early 19th century with a fashionably Greek Doric porch, was modernised about 1889. It was probably then that a shop (right) was converted to a doctor's surgery and given smart rusticated facing.

set back from the street, opposite the Woolstore. The new building was erected on the site of the brewery and other buildings which had developed behind the old inn to serve the coaching trade.[53]

Building and Restoration 1914–2006

The greatest impact on the built environment in both World Wars was the erection of mostly temporary structures associated with the army camps, and with the facilities that developed to serve them. Several of those structures may survive as outbuildings of houses but have yet to be identified. The building that became the office of Webbs Motor Caravans in High Street remained until it was rebuilt in the mid-20th century and some of the alterations made to the Woolstore in 1939–45 can still be seen. Among the few new houses built was the mock half-timbered Forde House on the east side of Chitterne Road, which in 1902 replaced a two-storey thatched cottage, perhaps 16th century in origin, that was destroyed by fire.

After 1945 the last open space on the north side of the High Street between the settlements was developed with local authority housing. Previously, in 1936–8, four pairs of plain red-brick council dwellings had been built beside New Road, outside and north of the village. In 1944 plans were drawn up by Warminster and Westbury RDC to build on the old cherry orchard between the two settlements, providing terraced and semi-detached houses of traditional two-storeyed, pitched-roofed form. A similar development took place in The Grove, south of High Street in Codford St Peter, in 1947–50. Some of the houses were built in brick but others, because of the post-war shortage of materials and labour, were built of concrete blocks. More houses, two blocks of cottage

Figure 38 Council houses
in The Grove. The plaque
records that they were
built by Warminster and
Westbury Rural District
Council which was justly
proud of this well-planned
extension to the village.

flats, and the primary school, built from 1969 and distinguishable
particularly by the weather-boarded panels so characteristic of
the period, were added off Cherry Orchard. Visually the housing
centred on the old orchard was an intentionally muted addition to
the village, low and set behind a strip of green which preserved the
illusion of a slight gap between the two Codfords.[54]

From 1945 until the 1970s other building work was mainly
limited to conversions of older properties. Both rectory houses
were sold as private houses. St Mary's, which had been sold in
1930, was split into two in about 1949 without being much altered,
and its stables, on the west side of Church Lane, were converted
into a separate house. Another important house was subjected to
extensive restoration by the former Wiltshire County Architect,
James Burford. In 1947–8 he returned the Old Manor House from
dereliction to something close to its 17th-century appearance and,
having occupied the house for several years, bought it in 1961. He

Figure 39 Cherry
Orchard. Council houses
which, like those in
The Grove, successfully
combine a traditional
terraced form with spare
modern details.

Figure 40 Quinton Close, off the Bury, one of the many sites in the centre of Codford exploited for new housing during the last 20 years. These homes were designed to resemble local Georgian houses.

also altered 102 Green Lane and in 1950 improved three cottages for the Wiltshire Cottage Improvement Trust.[55]

East Farm, which as the main house on the manor of Codford St Mary may have incorporated clues as to its early history, partly burned down in 1943 and was rebuilt in a more perfunctory fashion without its south-west wing; since 1987 its west front has been altered to resemble the rest of the house. Exceptionally, new farm buildings were erected at East Farm in 1953–4, whereas after 1945 elsewhere in the parish farm buildings, which became redundant as agricultural holdings were consolidated, were converted from their original use. The barn at Middle Farm became part of the house and the farmyard a garden soon after 1949, and buildings at Manor Farm had been altered by 1993. The remaining non-domestic buildings, including the redundant Victorian schools and the main Woolstore building, have been converted to residential use. The largest new house within the village was built by the Willoughby family, who in 1989 sold Overton House, and built themselves the individually-designed Rockworth House, large but traditional with Elizabethan-style chimneys and, unlike earlier prestigious houses in the village, discreetly sited behind the old kitchen garden walls of their former home.[56]

Such late 20th-century developments have been shaped by local planning restrictions. Although no part of Codford lies within a conservation area, its location in the Wylye Valley and, since 1983, within an Area of Outstanding Natural Beauty has led to constraints on building in the parish. Village policy limits for housing, developed by West Wiltshire District Council, are intended to restrict new developments to infill and brownfield sites and, although some have responded to the restrictions, others, such as housing along Green Lane, show that this policy has not always been adopted.[57]

THE WOOLSTORE: A BUILDING HISTORY

The Woolstore must have seemed an incongruous intruder on the south side of Codford St Peter's High Street when it appeared there in the mid-19th century. It is certainly a remarkable building, well worth highlighting here. Officially described as a woollen mill, it has never contained machinery for spinning or weaving cloth or for powering such machinery by steam, and it lies too far from the river to have been water-powered. The misidentification was an easy mistake to make. Externally the Woolstore shares many characteristics with the textile mills sited along the Wylye that took advantage of the wool produced on the downs above it, but it played a different role in the processing of wool. It was, in fact, a storehouse for fleece where wool was sorted and stored, awaiting collection by a dealer. The Woolstore forms only part of an extensive complex, on a site which stretches south from the High Street. The mansion house behind the Woolstore, now known as the Wool House, Wool Cottage to its east and the Woolstore's covered yard, now converted into the Woolstore Theatre, have all played a part in a complex and eventful history, whose most recent chapter has been the conversion of the Woolstore to flats in 2005 (see Chapter 4 and Panel 11).[58]

Study of the buildings and documents has revealed a considerable enterprise in the centre of a rural village in the middle of the 19th century. An entrepreneurial member of a local farming family acquired a pocket of land between the two villages which he cleared in order to build both the premises from which he ran his wool-sorting business and a substantial house in its own grounds for himself behind it. Some of his workers were housed in neighbouring properties that he owned.

Figure 41 The Woolstore, north elevation from the High Street.

The Woolstore stands hard against the road and partly hides a courtyard between it and the Wool House, which is set in a large well-treed garden stretching south towards the river. An adjacent range of single-storeyed buildings were stables and possibly grooms' and servants' quarters, since converted into several small dwellings. They stretch east to the Old Wool Cottage, a substantial house despite its name. The cottages adjoining the Woolstore's land that once belonged to the Woolstore's owners were sold off long ago.

In the following pages you can follow the method used to trace the history of the building. First, the building was examined in detail, inside and out, for evidence of how it was built, how it has grown, what style and building methods the owners chose for it and why, and how what we see today can be fleshed out with dates and personalities.

The Built Evidence

The Woolstore was built in two almost equal halves, although this is not apparent without careful scrutiny. Two rectangular three-storeyed ranges were built back to back, the back wall of the first range forming the partition between them. Each range has its own pitched roof, which meets in a central valley, and is covered in Welsh slates. The severe, symmetrical front of the north range facing the street makes an immediate impression. Despite the building's industrial purpose, it was carefully designed in classical style and built to a high standard to impress passers-by and, no doubt, to give confidence in the business. Like other local buildings, the Woolstore is built with a mixture of materials. Most of it is stone but, although the front wall is built of the local chalk, it has been faced in smooth red brick and given details in stone of better quality than the rest. The brick is laid in Flemish bond, a strong bond with bricks laid end-on showing headers alternating with those laid lengthways (stretcher). Popular since the 17th century, in Wiltshire Flemish bond was used in up to 49 per cent of all brickwork. Each cambered window head or arch is constructed with tapered bricks that have been gauged or rubbed by hand to fit, a time-consuming and therefore expensive process. The plinth at the base of the wall is greensand but the angles of the buildings, the window sills and the keystones over them are of stone that was easier to bring to a precise finish and which probably came from the Chilmark quarry in the Nadder valley south of the Wylye. Each angle has rusticated quoins – stone blocks with chamfered edges to emphasise the joints – a feature which originated in Renaissance Italy, is often seen in late 17th- and early 18th-century Wiltshire town houses, and was much used there in the 19th century. Bricks appear again on

Figure 42 The Woolstore, from the north-west, showing the back-to-back ranges of equal size, each with its own pitched roof meeting in a central valley.

the west front but the east wall of the north range is entirely built with squared greensand blocks, and so is the south wall, which was exposed until the south range was built against it. A barely perceptible joint on the east elevation shows where the south range was built against the north one; it sits within a recess made to take rainwater away from the valley between north and south roofs.[59]

The south elevation of the south range faced the Wool House where the owner of the Woolstore lived and so was given a decorative façade of the finer Chilmark stone. The style chosen here was not classical like the north front but simple Gothic, which had been popular for garden buildings since the 18th century. Both upper floors have pointed windows with Y-tracery of 13th-century type. All but the central one of the lower course were originally blind as the façade was merely a screen, intended to give an acceptable view from the Wool House without the workers being able to gaze out in return. Windows were unblocked, and new circular ones made, to light rooms during the conversion of the building to flats. The west face of the south range, which only overlooked a yard, is much more workmanlike, with a metal-framed casement lighting a sub-cellar at this end.

Timber was used for the internal structure and the windows, rather than the cast iron that, after 1796, was so often used in place of timber in textile factories and mills, where a combustible mix of raw materials, machine oil and lighted candles called for rigorous fire prevention measures. Presumably it was unnecessary as the Woolstore, unlike the large mill in Upton Lovell in the next parish and others along the Wylye valley, contained no textile machinery. Although timber formed an important part of the building, its use was regulated by an Act in 1774, which required all new buildings to incorporate measures to reduce the risk of fire starting and spreading. One requirement, followed on the north front of the Woolstore, restricted the use of projecting timberwork, which meant that windows had to be recessed in brick or stone reveals some four inches deep.

How the Building was Used

The building offers all kinds of clues about its use. There is no entrance on the street front and instead of ground-floor windows only round-arched ventilation louvres set in blank arches and blind doorways. Work demanding light and, at times, air seems to have been done on the upper floors where windows have glass and a central section with an opening sash. On the upper storeys at the east end of the building are doorways, used to dispatch the sacks of wool. Indeed the lintel of gauged stonework over the first-floor

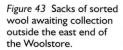

Figure 43 Sacks of sorted wool awaiting collection outside the east end of the Woolstore.

doorway is disfigured because of constant wearing away by pulley ropes. Over the second-floor doorway the beam from which the pulley hung is still in place and it seems from the way that the gauged stone arch of the doorway has been partially dismantled that the beam was added after the doorway was made. Perhaps workers originally had to carry the goods by way of ladders or to throw the sacks down.

Goods were received at the west end where there is a covered yard (now the Woolstore Theatre), screened from the street by a single-storeyed brick building with a slate roof, blind windows and a double-doored entrance. It served a practical purpose. Fleeces were brought to the Woolstore on carts, which originally stood in the open while their loads were transferred to the building for sorting. In rainy weather fleeces became wet, extremely heavy and so more difficult to manage. To avoid the problem, a covered yard was made to give protection to the fleeces and to the men handling them. Large south doors originally gave access for the carts (the runners for these can still be seen), whilst the entrance from the yard into the Woolstore was at the west end, behind what is now the stage of the theatre, to the right of the west wall. Here there were big cantilever doors and the fleeces were thrown down into the basement, to be hoisted up. The building of the yard seems to have consolidated a flow of work which involved the raw materials entering on the west, being hauled to the upper floors where the wool was sorted and the finished goods being dispatched in sacks through the doors at the east end (see Panel 11).[60]

Inside the Woolstore

The interior tells us little about what working life was like. There is no trace of where the wool sorters sat at their benches or of how the wool was stored. At the west end of the ground floor a partitioned section was probably used as an office and was heated by a brick hearth, its segmental-arched head supported on an iron band typical of the mid-19th century.

The most eloquent survivals are the roofs of the two parallel ranges, which help us to determine how the building developed (see Panel 4). Each roof has been constructed in a different way, the north one with king-post construction, the south one with queen-posts. The walling suggests that the north range was built before the south one and so do the roofs. Perhaps the queen-post type of roof was chosen for the later range because it was cheaper to construct or because by then it was commonly used locally. It was not selected for its usual purpose of bridging wider than average spans, for example of a large barn, because here spans of each range are equal.

How the Site Developed

Examination of the building has shown that the Woolstore developed gradually. With the clues the building itself has provided, we can make more sense of what documents and maps tell us about the site and the group of buildings on it. The earliest clear evidence dates from 1810 when a close examination of the Enclosure Award map for Codford St Peter reveals that, where the Woolstore now

Map 12 Part of the 1810 Enclosure Award map for Codford St Peter. The red blocks represent dwelling houses and other buildings are hatched in black. The cottages that were demolished when the Woolstore was built are outlined in yellow.

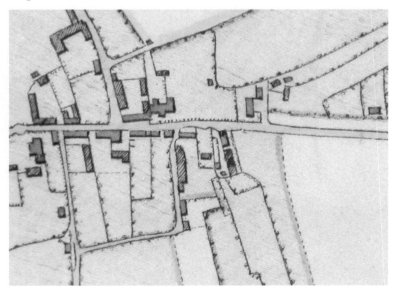

stands, there was only an irregular row of cottages. The same map also shows that the land on which the Woolstore properties were eventually built was then divided into four long closes, bounded on the north by the buildings fronting the High Street, which included Manor House Cottage and 103 High Street, on the west by Doughty Lane, and on the east and south by a lane which ran south from the High Street and turned sharply west to meet Doughty Lane. When the land was purchased, though Manor House Cottage and 103 High Street retained their gardens, they lost their closes.[61]

The first owners of the Woolstore were called Raxworthy. As substantial local landowners they were first recorded in Codford in 1824, when James Raxworthy paid 1s. for exonerated tax which, in records of 1825 and beyond, turns out to be tax on a house (see Chapter 4). By deduction we can identify this house with the Wool House, which he probably built about 1823–4. We can be certain that he owned the Wool House by 1840 and had built the Woolstore, the 'wool shop' described in schedule 139 of the Tithe Award. Raxworthy also owned other properties on either side of 139 (shown as schedules 136, 140 and 141), as well as a cottage and land tucked between those scheduled as 149 and 138, and 135 which he leased to William Bennett. He also had property in Codford St Mary. We can see from the 1840 Tithe Award map that the 'wool shop' was the north range of the present Woolstore. It is shown on the site of the earlier cottages as a single, narrow, rectangular build-ing, occupying the northern half of its present footprint.[62]

The southern range had been added by 1869 and was followed by the covered yard, which was not included on a sale catalogue plan of

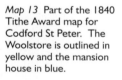

Map 13 Part of the 1840 Tithe Award map for Codford St Peter. The Woolstore is outlined in yellow and the mansion house in blue.

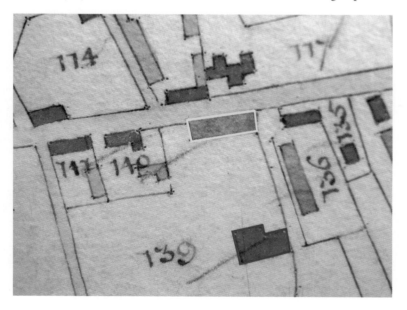

Map 14 Plan accompanying a sale catalogue of 1869. The Woolstore is outlined in yellow, the Wool House in blue.

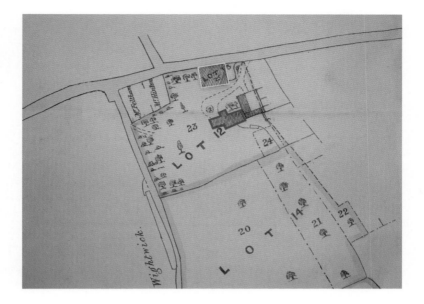

1869 but is represented on the 1886 Ordnance Survey map. There is evidence, too, that there was a second woolstore, mentioned as being of 'timber and slate' in an abstract of title of 1909. It has disappeared but may have been the small structure tucked into the angle between the back of the Woolstore and the covered courtyard that was drawn on a plan of 1927 and a map of 1965.[63]

Map 15 Part of the 1st edition Ordnance Survey map (1886) showing Codford St Peter. The Woolstore is outlined in yellow, Wool House in blue and the Old Wool House Cottage in purple.

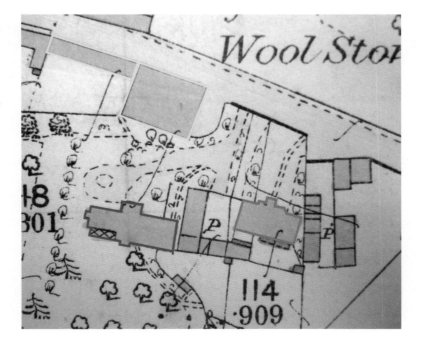

Roofing the Woolstore

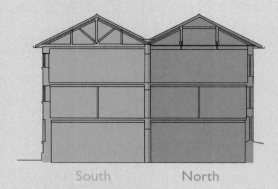

South   North

Documents suggest that the Woolstore was constructed in two halves, a supposition confirmed by examining the structure itself. One of the key pieces of evidence is that the roofs over the south and north halves are quite different. The earlier, south range has a king post roof, the north one a queen post roof. Both roofs are 19th-century versions of traditional forms, constructed with mechanically sawn softwood, reinforced with iron, rather than with the handcut and pegged oak and elm of earlier Codford roofs.

The main elements of each roof are the trusses which support all the other timbers. A truss is a triangular framework composed of the main horizontal tiebeam spanning between the tops of the walls, inclined timbers called principals, and intermediate timbers that keep the framework rigid, the main ones in this case being a king post or queen post. Used in series along the length of the roof, the trusses support the longitudinal timbers (purlins and ridge pieces) that carry the roof covering.

In a king post truss the king post rises vertically from the centre of the tiebeam. The head of the post is usually enlarged into a jowl to be capable of supporting both the ends of the principals and the ridge piece (here an upright ridge board) at the apex of the roof. The principals tend to sag and so are usually supported midway down by struts that spring from the kingpost. In the Woolstore a cast iron bolt has been added to strengthen the tenon joint between tiebeam and post and so prevent the tiebeam collapsing under the force of the upward thrust of the principals.

A conventional queen post truss has a pair of queen posts, placed symmetrically and rising vertically from a tiebeam to support purlins or horizontally set plates, which rest on the collar that connects the principals near the apex. Struts rather than posts rise to the collar and do not directly support the purlins. The Woolstore roof is a hybrid type in which the queen posts support not purlins or plates but the head of the principals, which stop short of the apex. A strainer beam holds the posts apart. Post and tiebeam are held together by a stirrup, a wrought iron strap fastened by wrought iron and timber fixings (dogs, gibs, cotters). From this example it is clear that not all roofs conform to the conventional types shown in standard books on timber-framing.

The drawings opposite show how the elements of the Woolstore roofs are assembled. Other elements used in their construction are:

Common rafters: rafters of uniform size regularly spaced in couples along the length of the roof. Supported by the purlins and supporting the roof covering
Strut: a vertical or diagonally set timber, used to brace the truss
Trenched purlin: a purlin which sits in a trench cut across the back of a principal.

Matthew Bristow

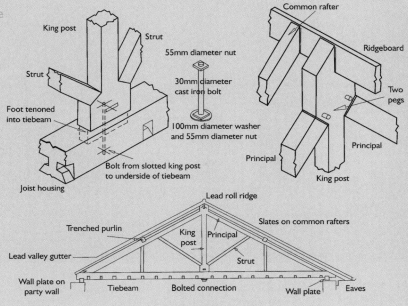

King post

Strut

Strut

Foot tenoned
into tiebeam

Joist housing

55mm diameter nut

30mm diameter
cast iron bolt

100mm diameter washer
and 55mm diameter nut

Bolt from slotted king post
to underside of tiebeam

Common rafter

Ridgeboard

Two
pegs

Principal

Principal

King post

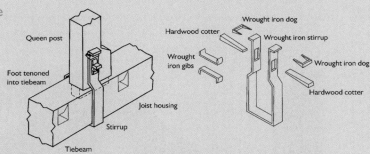

Lead roll ridge

Trenched purlin

Slates on common rafters

Lead valley gutter

King
post

Principal

Strut

Wall plate on
party wall

Tiebeam

Bolted connection

Wall plate

Eaves

KING POST TRUSS

North range

Queen post

Foot tenoned
into tiebeam

Joist housing

Stirrup

Tiebeam

Hardwood cotter

Wrought
iron gibs

Wrought iron dog

Wrought iron stirrup

Wrought iron dog

Hardwood cotter

QUEEN POST TRUSS

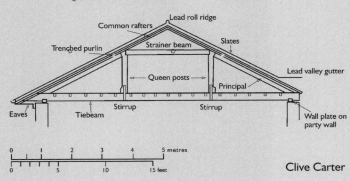

Lead roll ridge

Common rafters

Strainer beam

Slates

Trenched purlin

Queen posts

Principal

Lead valley gutter

Eaves

Tiebeam

Stirrup

Stirrup

Wall plate on
party wall

0   1   2   3   4   5 metres

0   5   10   15 feet

Clive Carter

Figure 44 The mansion house, known as the Wool House, was built *c*.1823 and extended in 1869. It enjoyed views of a large garden overlooking the Wylye Valley.

The Wool House and Old Wool House Cottage

In 1840 the plain classical Wool House had an L-plan, but by the time it was put up for sale in 1869 there was not only a northern extension, but a range of outbuildings, running north to south, appears to have been incorporated into the premises and perhaps partially rebuilt. By 1886 this ancillary range extended behind what is now Old Wool House Cottage, which in 1869 and possibly before

Figure 45 The north front of the owner's house faced the Woolstore which was given a façade of high-quality local stone and Gothic windows.

was an independent property. In 1810 there had been a small cottage there within a small garden. By 1840 the depiction of it on the map had changed shape and the cottage may have been rebuilt on a north–south alignment. Cottage and garden belonged to James Raxworthy but were rented by John Foley from William Bennett, who held the lease from Raxworthy. By 1886 it had either been greatly enlarged or entirely rebuilt as a large house, most of which still stands, though perhaps altered to the south and west. [64]

Changes of Name

The Wool House was not so called until 1967. It was known genteelly as The Beeches in 1861, and there are still several magnificent copper beech trees growing in the grounds, possibly those planted in the mid-19th century. In 1929 Colonel Sneyd, who had bought both Woolstore and Wool House in 1926, renamed the house Bradwell Grange, after his much grander family home in Staffordshire, and later deeds refer to names conjuring up its river valley associations – Flying Goose Furlong (1950), Gray's Mead (1963, 1964) and Flying Goose Farm.[65]

The Wool Sorters' Houses

The garden containing the outbuildings later incorporated into the Wool House property also had a pair of cottages fronting the High Street, which, in 1840, were rented out by James Raxworthy

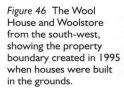

Figure 46 The Wool House and Woolstore from the south-west, showing the property boundary created in 1995 when houses were built in the grounds.

to Charles Shingle and John Penny, both wool sorters. Next door to
the east lived Mary Everley and possibly her brother and his wife;
he was a skinner. The cottages are schedule 136 on the Tithe Award
map. To the west of the Woolstore, the present Manor House
Cottage was uninhabited at the time of the 1841 census, though
the previous year had seen William Brown and George Lever in
residence. Beyond them, at present 103 High Street, lived Thomas
Swayne and his family and Robert Foot; both these men were wool
sorters. So it would seem that Raxworthy gathered his work force
about him, putting them into cottages close to his own property,
wherever possible. [66]

Chapter 3 | Lords and Landowners

This chapter is concerned with the ownership of Codford, principally with discovering and describing the owners of the various manors which have existed within the two parishes. The term 'manor' in this context relates not to a house – indeed Codford has never had a building which can truly be described as a manor house – but to a relationship. That relationship, between landowner, tenantry and land, sometimes existed before the Conquest, but was formulated as integral to the political and social system by Norman legislators, and deemed to include every landholding by the compilers of Domesday Book. Although its significance waned after the Middle Ages, and lordship of a manor gradually drifted away from ownership of an estate, the institution remained significant over much of rural England until the 18th or 19th century.

A manor was therefore a territorial and an economic unit, which belonged to someone – the lord of the manor – and within which people exploited the natural resources of its territory. Those people might be employed directly by the lord, or might recompense him, by regular or irregular payments, or by labour and other services, for the use of his land. Conduct on the manor was dictated by rules known as customs, which varied from one manor to another, and was controlled by manorial courts. The manor therefore was a miniature commonwealth which permeated many aspects of its members' lives. Here the concern is with ownership, with the lords of the manors, and their impact on local government. The way manorial arrangements affected agriculture is discussed in chapter 4.

Charting the descent of a manor provides information about ownership which underpins and can help to explain the history of any community. Like compiling a pedigree, however, it involves specialist knowledge and familiarity with archaic and obscure legal expressions. In the paragraphs that follow the technicalities have been kept to a minimum, and the manorial descents are summarised in tabular form alongside the narrative commentary.

It is important to realise that manors need not coincide with parishes, and indeed may not represent discrete geographical entities. They were frequently divided and sometimes reunited. They often had more than one layer of ownership, from the king (nominal owner of everything), through an overlord, to one or more tenant and sub-tenant, who actually possessed the manor. It is very

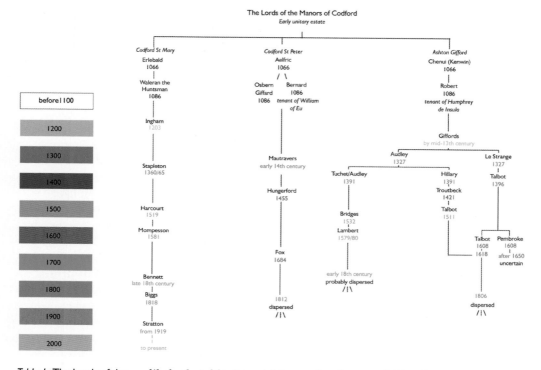

The Lords of the Manors of Codford
Early unitary estate

Codford St Mary	*Codford St Peter*	*Ashton Gifford*
Erlebald	Aelfric	Chenui (Kenwin)
1066	1066	1066
	/ \	
Waleran the	Osbern Bernard	Robert
Huntsman	Giffard 1086	1086
1086	1086 *tenant of William*	*tenant of Humphrey*
	of Eu	*de Insula*
Ingham		
1203		Giffords
		by mid-13th century

| before1100 |
| 1200 |
| 1300 |
| 1400 |
| 1500 |
| 1600 |
| 1700 |
| 1800 |
| 1900 |
| 2000 |

Table 1 The Lords of the Manor of Codford. For the sources used in this table and throughout this chapter, see the Land Ownership section in the Bibliography and Sources.

likely that, like its neighbours Stockton and Sherrington, Codford was originally a substantial unitary estate. By 1066, however, it had been divided into what appears to have been three separate holdings, corresponding to the parish of Codford St Mary and the tithings of Codford St Peter and Ashton Gifford, both in the parish of Codford St Peter (see Chapter 5). After the Conquest, there were further changes. The manor of Codford St Peter was divided and then reunited, while Ashton Gifford was divided, subdivided and partially reunited. For much of their history none of these estates had a resident manorial lord, and many of Codford's owners have been distant magnates with little or no local knowledge (see Table 1). Their main impact on the estate will have been through their stewards and the conduct of the manorial courts, discussed below, where the tenants will in many ways have regulated their own affairs.

CODFORD ST MARY

For at least 940 years, and perhaps much longer, most land in Codford St Mary has belonged to a single estate, which can be traced passing through some forty owners, from an Anglo-Saxon named Erlebald in 1066 to Josh Stratton, the present owner of East Farm (see Table 1). During such a long span of time there

have inevitably been losses and gains of land, and some land lost
has been regained; and there have been periods when lordship of
the manor was distinct from ownership of the estate. But overall,
Codford St Mary, in common with some other Wylye Valley
manors, exhibits a remarkable degree of continuity. In particular,
East Farm has remained the chief house or home farm from at least
the early 17th century and very probably long before that.

After the Norman Conquest the manor was one of 16 in
Wiltshire given by King William I to Waleran the huntsman (see
Chapter 1). Codford St Mary passed to his descendants for more
than five centuries, until it was sold in 1581. During this time
the male line failed three times, in 1200–1, 1344 and 1466, and
on each occasion a daughter passed the manor to her husband,
so that the family name changed from Waleran, to Ingham, to
Stapleton, and finally to Harcourt. This chain was broken by Sir
Walter Harcourt in 1581, who sold the manor and most of the
estate to the Mompessons. They remained lords of the manor until
the later 18th century, but in the early 1620s the then head of the
family, Giles, who had been impeached and heavily fined for extor-
tion, was forced to sell a large part of his estate to the Topp family
of Stockton. In the late 18th century that estate was sold to the
Bennett family (of Pythouse near Tisbury) who also acquired the
remaining Mompesson interest and became thereby lords of the
manor and the largest landowners in the parish. In 1818 they sold
their estate to Harry Biggs, who was lord of the manor of neighbouring Stockton, and who also purchased land in Codford St
Peter when the manor was sold by Lord Ilchester. The Biggs family
continued to hold a large estate of over 1,300 acres in Codford,

Figure 47 Sir Giles
Mompesson depicted as
an extortioner in a hostile
tract, 1621.

Figure 48 Tomb in St Mary's church, Lydiard Tregoze to Sir Giles Mompesson and his wife Katherine, erected after Lady Mompesson's death in 1633.

mostly worked as a single farm (East Farm) until 1919, when it was put up for sale by the then owner H.W. Yeatman-Biggs, bishop of Coventry. In 1921 East Farm was bought by J.M. Stratton, scion of a famous Wiltshire farming dynasty, and now forms part of a local estate of some 3,400 acres still in the hands of the family.

The impact of these landowners on the parish has varied considerably. The medieval lords were all absentee and probably had little personal connection with Codford. The Inghams, for example, in possession from 1254 to the 1360s, were a Norfolk soldiering family, and the Stapletons who followed them came from Yorkshire. Almost certainly their principal contact with it would have been through stewards who would have come from time to time to collect dues and to preside at the manorial court. But after the 1581 sale all the owning families had close connections with nearby places in the Wylye Valley and so, if absentee landlords in the sense that they did not live on the manor, were nevertheless familiar with Codford themselves, or were closely related to people who knew the area well. The Mompessons, a distinguished Wiltshire family

Table 2

The Mompessons and their connections with Codford

Those members of the family connected with Codford are in bold

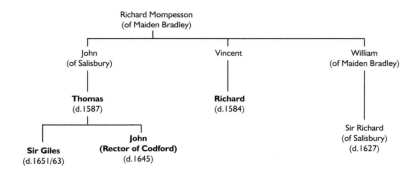

established at Bathampton and nearby in Corton in Boyton, had particularly close associations with Codford in the late 16th and early 17th centuries. Richard (d. 1584), the first to establish himself in the parish, was a member of a cadet branch of the family and was succeeded by his cousin Thomas from Bathampton. A grand tomb in Codford St Mary where in the earlier 17th century one of Thomas's sons was rector (see Chapter 6 and Table 2) probably commemorates him. Later landowning families included the Topps, Biggs and Strattons, who lived at Stockton, and the Bennetts, who were related to a landowning family at Norton Bavant (see Table 2). In the 20th century, under the Strattons, East Farm has been integrated into a well-established locally based agricultural business.[67]

CODFORD ST PETER

What became the manor of Codford St Peter constituted only part of St Peter's parish, as Ashton Gifford's manorial history was quite separate. When first encountered, in Domesday Book, there were two estates in this part of Codford St Peter, although the Domesday entries suggest that before the Conquest they may have been a single estate, belonging to Aelfric, which was then divided more or less equally between two Norman recipients, Osbern Giffard and William of Eu.

The two post-Conquest estates remained nominally distinct until 1330. The Giffard family retained their portion (apart from a period of confiscation, 1322-7, during Edward II's reign) until then, and were related by marriage to the Mautravers family, owner of the other estate from 1243 or earlier. Both the Giffards and the Mautravers were baronial families with portfolios of land extending far beyond Wiltshire, and no particular connection with Codford. Members of both families played prominent roles in royal and national politics during the 13th and 14th centuries, and were temporarily deprived of their estates. As at St Mary's, almost certainly their main contact with the parish would have been through their stewards.

In 1330 both estates came into the possession of Sir John Mautravers (see Table 1). Thereafter, the main focus of the manor seems to have been around St Peter's church on either side of the main road, the house now known as the Manor House being the chief house of the manor where the steward presumably stayed. The Mautravers retained ownership of the reunited manor until 1455, when, through a widow who had remarried, it passed to

Map 16 Detail from estate map of the manor of Codford St Peter 1809.

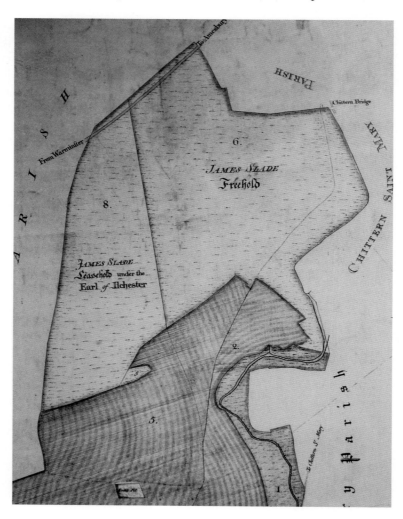

Figure 49 Tomb of Sir Edward Hungerford, lord of the manor of Codford St Peter 1607-48, and his wife, in Farleigh Hungerford Castle chapel. Sir Edward died childless and was the uncle of the spendthrift Sir Edward, last of the Codford Hungerfords, who was forced to sell the manor in 1684.

one of the largest of the West Country magnate families. The Hungerfords' principal seat was Farleigh Hungerford (Somerset) near Trowbridge, but they also had an important base nearby at Heytesbury. Theirs was a colourful family history, including murder, incest, treachery, execution, disgrace and bankruptcy, but they also possessed great wealth and wielded considerable influence in the Heytesbury area, and Wiltshire generally. Their acquisition of Codford St Peter, the result of the Mautravers heiress, Eleanor, marrying as her third husband Walter, Lord Hungerford, was controversial. He predeceased her, and it was claimed that the reversion should have gone to her son by her first marriage. But the Hungerfords retained possession after her death, forfeited all their property in 1461 after supporting Henry VI during the Wars of the Roses, and only recovered Codford in 1485. Thereafter it remained in the family, though rarely passing from father to son, until Sir Edward Hungerford, an unsuccessful politician with extravagant tastes, was forced to sell the manor to pay off debts in 1684.

The buyer was Sir Stephen Fox, a financial expert in government service, who from humble origins at Farley near Salisbury had accrued staggering wealth which he used to purchase estates in Wiltshire and Somerset. When he died in his 90th year in 1716, he left Codford St Peter to a son, Stephen (then still a child), whose own son, Henry Fox Strangways, earl of Ilchester, sold it almost a century later, in 1812. At this point the estate was broken up.

ASHTON GIFFORD

Of the Codford manors it is the westernmost, Ashton Gifford, that has had the most convoluted manorial history (see Table 1). This is because, with the failure of the male line after 1322, it was divided in 1327 between two heirs, and each of the resulting halves was subdivided, in 1391 and 1608. To further complicate matters, two of the resulting 'quarters' (from different halves) were combined after 1618, and the descent of the other two cannot be traced after 1650 and 1733 respectively. What remained of the manor in 1806 was broken up and sold.

The intact manor, before the 1327 division, can be identified with a Domesday estate which at the Conquest had belonged to Chenui (or Kenwin), and by 1086 was one of 27 Wiltshire possessions of Humphrey de l'Isle. Many of these properties descended to the Dunstanville family and formed a portfolio of land (or barony) centred on Castle Combe, near Chippenham. In 1086 the manor was tenanted. By 1243 John Mautravers was tenant, and there was a sub-tenant, his brother-in-law, Sir Ellis Giffard, each of whom also held half the manor of Codford St Peter. Whatever the niceties of feudal tenure it was clearly the Giffords who were in charge of Ashton, and therefore added to it their name, in order to distinguish it from other Wiltshire Ashtons. They lost it in 1322 when John Gifford was hanged without a male heir. In 1327, when his property was restored to the family, it was distributed to descendants of his married daughters.

After 1327 one portion of Gifford's holdings, a half and then (from 1391) a quarter of the manor, descended through members of the Audley family until 1532, when it was sold to Henry Bridges. His grandson sold it again, in 1579–80, to Edmund Lambert, in whose family it continued until 1733 or later. The other quarter created by the 1391 division descended by marriage to a family named Troutbeck, and in 1511 to John Talbot, a kinsman of the earls of Shrewsbury. In 1618 John's great-grandson George became earl of Shrewsbury, and his Ashton estate passed into the earldom, where it remained until the 1806 sale.

Meanwhile the other half portion created by the 1327 division passed much more rapidly, after two generations in 1396, to the Talbot family, and became a possession of the earls of Shrewsbury in 1442. It might be expected, therefore, that three-quarters of Ashton Gifford manor would have been reunited in 1618, but that did not happen. Ten years earlier, in 1608, the earldom strand was divided, half remaining with the earl. The other half was inherited by a daughter, Mary, who was wife of William, earl of Pembroke. It remained with the Pembroke family of Wilton House until later in the 17th century, after which the descent is lost.

THE NEW ORDER

The manorial owners were important to Codford as ultimate beneficiaries of whatever the community could produce, and, through their courts, as controllers of who farmed the land, who lived where, and how residents conducted themselves. But most were remote, with no recognised presence in Codford. The men and women of real local substance and influence were their principal tenants, and several tenant families built up considerable estates of their own. Augmented by land purchases when the moribund manors were broken up in the 19th century, their successes and failures have shaped the farming estates of Victorian and later Codford.

It was possible, with the manorial lord's acquiescence, to build up a freehold estate in the Middle Ages, and in Codford this was achieved by the Hungerford family's receiver-general, Thomas Tropnell. Beginning in 1449, he acquired from his employer land and annuities in Codford St Peter and Ashton Gifford, and then purchased closes in Codford St Mary from the manorial lord. His family continued to hold the small estate after his death in 1488, until it was divided between daughters when his grandson died in 1548.

Other land was granted away by medieval owners for religious purposes. Such was a two-acre plot given in 1317 by Oliver de Ingham, lord of Codford St Mary, to Henry de Mareys to establish a hermitage, including a chapel, on a spur of the downs east of the

Figure 50 Likeness of Thomas Tropnell from a wall painting in his house, Great Chalfield Manor.

village. A few years later, in 1324, land in St Mary's was given to
Longleat Priory to maintain four chaplains in the church at Hill
Deverill. After the Dissolution most of this land eventually (in
1632) reverted to the manorial owner, but a part remained separate,
and was sold in 1680 to a member of a local family, John Ingram.

The Ingrams, along with the Hintons and the Slades, were
families recorded in Codford during the 16th and 17th centuries
who were beginning to accumulate estates of their own. There
were Ingrams in both parishes. The Codford St Mary family had
accumulated a small farm of freehold and copyhold land by 1790,
which passed to and was extended by the Revd James Ingram, a
scholar and antiquary, until the estate was dispersed at his death in
1850. The Codford St Peter branch of the Ingrams were important
farmers by 1714, with a freehold estate in 1736. Four Ingrams
owned land there in 1803, and their largest holding, of about 166
acres, passed by marriage to another local landowner, William
Hubbard, in about 1829.

Philip and John Hinton were Ashton Gifford tenants in 1657,
and their descendants amassed a holding of land there and in both
Codfords during the 18th and 19th centuries. What remained in
1856 was sold to another local farmer, James Raxworthy. His farm
in 1839 extended to nearly 850 acres in 1839, of which he owned
more than a third. He continued to buy land, too recklessly in the
event, not only from the Hintons, but also from James Ingram
and Harry Biggs of St Peter's, until his mortgagors foreclosed and
sold the estate. The purchaser of much of this land was William
Bennett, by then a major farmer and landowner in Codford St
Mary, whose estate, in 1882 when he died and it was broken up,
was valued at £44,000.

The Slade family, like the Hintons, had long been in Codford
– an Edward Slade was leasing East Farm, St Mary's in the 1560s
and 1570s. James Slade had increased his 100-acre holding in St
Peter's in 1776 to 432 acres there and in Ashton Gifford by 1810,
with a further 161 acres leased. This estate was greatly augmented
by his descendants until in 1877, when it totalled about 941 acres,
it was sold to William Chisman. This, with a further 178 acres purchased from the owner of Ashton Gifford House, John Ravenhill,
went to create the Manor Farm estate, which Chisman sold to the
Collins family, the present owners, in 1913.

The vicissitudes of many smaller landholdings in Codford
during the 19th and 20th centuries could be recited to illustrate
the widening of ownership following the break up of the large
manorial estates. But only one further estate is of great significance,
and that is Ashton Gifford. The first purchaser of the earl of
Shrewsbury's estate, in 1806, may have embarked on building his

mansion there, but over-reached himself and was imprisoned for debt in 1818. One of his mortgagors, William Hubbard, who had married into the Ingram family of Codford in 1809, took possession of the house in 1815, and completed it. After his death in 1831 the estate had a succession of owners, including briefly James Raxworthy, then Wadham Locke, who remodelled the house and created the park, then from 1850 John Ravenhill. A prominent figure in Wiltshire society, Ravenhill served as high sheriff in 1870, but after his death in 1878 house and estate were separated. The house has since had periods of use as a school and as a private house.

MANOR GOVERNMENT

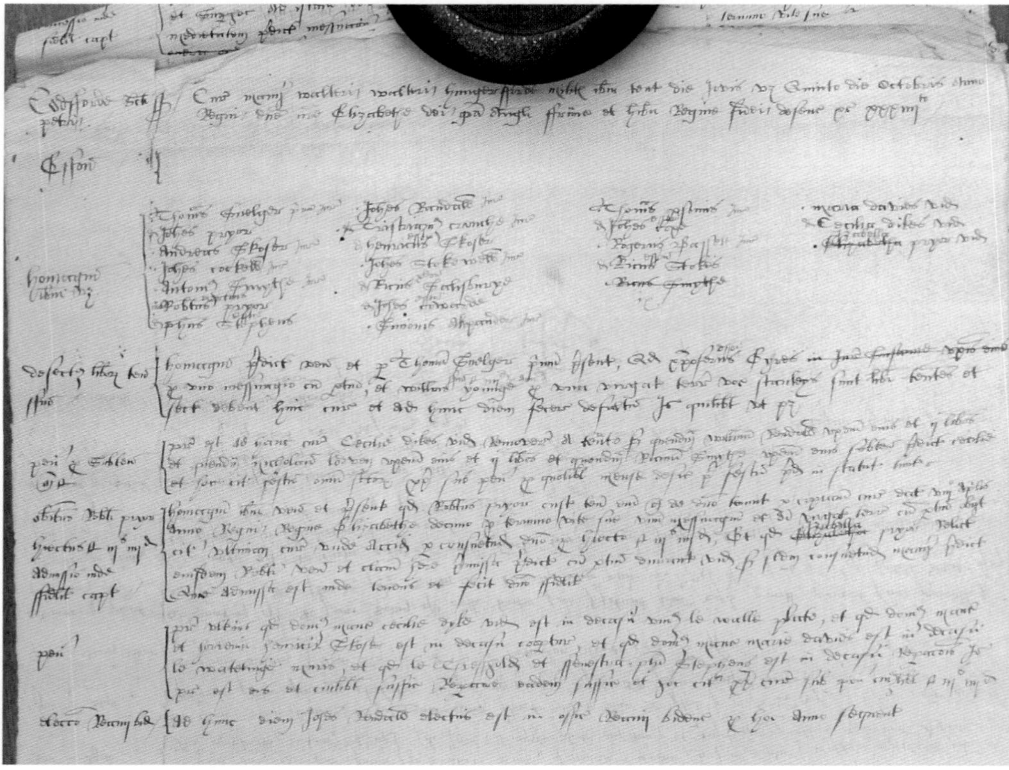

Figure 51 Court Roll of Codford St Peter from 1592.

Codford St Mary was holding manorial courts by 1282, although no court records are known to survive before the 17th century. From the scanty evidence it appears that all tenants were required to attend, and the court met irregularly up to five times each year, as and when business demanded. It continued to meet until the 19th century, but where is unknown. Codford St Peter's courts, first referred to in 1327, were being held twice a year in 1466–7, and in spring and autumn in the 16th century. All tenants had to attend and were fined if absent. After 1684 sessions became less regular, meeting generally once each year, or when required, and in some years not at all. The court house where meetings were usually held was accidentally burnt down in 1728 and thereafter the court met at the *George Inn*. It functioned until the 1860s.[68]

Ashton Gifford's courts were more complicated, and business for some tenants was at times transacted in the courts of neighbouring Sherrington or Boyton. A court for customary tenants was recorded in 1327, and courts were sometimes held for all tenants even after the manor had been divided. In 1633 and 1678 separate courts were held for tenants of the earl of Pembroke's manor, but no later courts for either of Ashton Gifford's manors are recorded.[69]

The main recorded business of all the courts related to the tenure of land, as holdings were surrendered to the manor and regranted to other tenants. Transfers of this kind generally occurred when a tenant or a named 'life' died, and then a fee had to be paid to the manorial lord. (see Panel 5). It was important that the executors of a deceased tenant did not lose the produce of his final year, and from 1609 onwards strict rules were regularly recited in Codford St Peter's court. The handover was to take place in stages after the tenant's death, first the fallow land and meadow (in March), then the barns (August), finally the entire holding (October).[70]

Buildings were also a court matter. In St Peter's court in 1524, for example, a ruinous cottage called 'Stockhouse', a stable and cottage called 'Davy's', and a cottage kitchen which was collapsing into the road, were all reported for repair. In St Mary's a court ordered that a house built on the manorial waste without permission should be either pulled down or confiscated for the manorial lord's use. In 1654 the same court heard that the manorial pound was in disrepair, whereas in 1761 and 1763 the tenants of St Peter's complained to their court that there was no pound, and they desired the lord to erect one.[71]

Management of the common pasture and other shared facilities was a major concern in all the Codford manor courts. At Ashton Gifford in 1621 the tenants complained of the damage done by unringed pigs belonging both to their own manor and to tenants of Codford St Peter. In St Mary's, as probably in each manor, the court provided a forum through which lord and tenant controlled and regulated land use, maintained the integrity of boundaries, and penalised those who encroached upon, appropriated or blocked access to common land. A particular concern in St Mary's court in 1640 and 1649 was that the lessee of the manor farm denied the tenants materials needed to maintain the water meadows.[72]

In charge of proceedings at manorial courts were stewards employed by the lord. The names of many Codford stewards are known, and it is clear that several held office for long periods. Most did not live in Codford, but travelled around the various manors of a particular lord – which in the case of the Hungerford family in the 17th century were numerous – and were paid a stipend and expenses to preside over the courts. The principal resident official was the hayward, who was responsible for supervising hay, wood and pasture. No hayward is recorded for St Mary's manor, but in 1330–1 one hayward served both St Peter's and Ashton Gifford. In the 18th century the St Peter's court elected its hayward, and the names of several are recorded. How they were chosen before this is unknown. Also on St Peter's manor the court elected two affeerors (who fixed the penalties for offences), a sheep reeve and a gamekeeper.[73]

Copyhold Tenure

Anyone exploring the history of tenants and tenure in a village will very soon encounter the word 'copyhold'. The 'copy' by which such land or other property was held was an extract copied from the manorial court roll, which recorded the admission of a tenant to his or her holding. This copy therefore acted as the equivalent of a title deed, describing when, where, for how long, for what payment and under what conditions a tenant might enjoy his possession, according to the customs of the manor.

On many Wiltshire manors copyholders, also known as customary tenants because their tenure was regulated by manorial custom, formed the largest group of tenants. They were ranked below freeholders (who were largely independent of manorial control) and leaseholders, whose tenure was based on a fixed term and payment of rent. Leasehold, which was not governed by manorial custom, gradually replaced copyhold from the 16th century, and copyhold was abolished altogether in 1922.

Copyhold was perpetuated by inheritance or by 'lives' (leases were often held for the life of one or more lessees). Although rent was generally paid the major expenses were the substantial payments (known as an entry fines and heriots) which the manorial lord exacted on his tenant's embarking on or inheriting the tenancy. If a copyhold or leasehold was on 'lives', generally three named individuals, the tenure could, if the lord agreed, be extended by adding a life when one of the three died – this too incurred a large one-off payment.

For the local historian the importance of copyhold tenure is not just that it was the way of life for most small farmers and village residents for several centuries, affecting their status, security and readiness to look after their homes. It has also resulted in extensive records – copies of court roll, court rolls themselves, manorial extents and surveys – which of necessity had to describe the heirs or lives. And so they give clues about many village families and their circumstances, such as longevity, relationships to each other and lineage through generations.

A late 18th-century example of copyhold tenure (in English) from a Codford St Peter court roll. These documents describe how manorial custom governed the agreements between landowner and tenant. Before the 18th century they were usually written in Latin.

Chapter 4

Making a Living

The principal activity in Codford has always been agriculture. For centuries the Wylye Valley was an area of sheep farming and barley production, where the sheep were used to dung the land which grew the barley, which in turn was sent to Warminster market for use in brewing. The sheep indigenous to the area were the Wiltshire Horn, a slender, long-legged breed, aptly suited to the steep downs. This mixed economy can be detected from the first written record, the entries relating to Codford in the great survey known as Domesday Book.

The importance of sheep in the area, however, also encouraged industrial activity based on their wool. Weaving and spinning long had a local importance and in the 19th century local entrepreneurs developed an important wool-sorting industry in the village.

FROM THE LAND

The Domesday Record

The Domesday survey is an extraordinary and unprecedented document. It was commissioned by William I at the end of his life to assess the nation's economic worth in 1086 and compare it with that of twenty years earlier when he had conquered England. The work of the surveyors in counting, valuing and measuring everything of potential value to the Crown was meticulous, if at times puzzling and enigmatic. For most places it is the earliest written record of how, at local level, our Anglo-Saxon and Norman ancestors operated. This is true of Codford. From the world of the prehistoric and early farmers, glimpsed only from archaeological remains, Domesday Book leads us towards another world, that of medieval and later agriculture, seen in accounts, surveys and minutes of meetings.

Codford has four entries in Domesday Book, one for what became St Mary's, one for Ashton Gifford and two for St Peter's (see Panel 6). A translation of the actual wording, with explanations, is given in the Panel, and from what we read there it is possible to draw some conclusions. All four estates had arable land, meadow and pasture, and there were two mills for grinding corn – one for St Mary's, the other shared between St Peter's and

Figure 52 A medieval
water mill, depicted
in the Luttrell Psalter,
*c.*1320-40.

Ashton. The meadowland was undoubtedly then, as later, along the
northern bank of the Wylye, and much of the pasture would have
been on Codford's downland. Each of the four estates cultivated
its arable land in two portions, the demesne or home farm, and
the tenantry. The demesne was farmed directly by the servants (in
effect slaves) of the landowner; he also owned the tenantry's land,
for which they paid him a rent based on labour and other services.

For tax purposes St Mary's and Ashton Gifford were reckoned
the same size, six hides apiece. The land of both was divided equally
between the lord and the tenantry, and both had increased in value
since 1066. But St Mary's had more tenant families – 13 compared
with Ashton's seven – and a greater extent of pasture. It had a mill
to itself, arable for six ploughteams compared with Ashton's four,
and was consequently worth twice as much. The two St Peter's
estates together were only computed at three hides, although they
supported nine tenant families and had arable for four ploughteams. Their combined value had fallen slightly since 1066.[74]

The Arable Fields

The farming regime described in abbreviated form by Domesday
Book can be elaborated from later records. Throughout the Middle
Ages and until the 19th century each estate's arable land was laid
out in large open fields divided into blocks of strips known as
furlongs. Every tenant cultivated the strips allotted to him, as well
as working a proportion of his week on the strips belonging to the
landowner's demesne farm. The level of such service demanded
from tenants varied, and nothing is known of the practice on the
St Peter's manors. But for Ashton Gifford it was set out in detail in
1299 when the landowner died, and for St Mary's in 1310 under
similar circumstances.[75]

In Ashton Gifford there was a clear grading of society. The four
tenants of the smaller holdings had to work alternate days on
the demesne land (excluding the religious festival periods), and
during the harvest months of August and September they were
required there every day. The value of their work was reckoned
at a farthing a day, which suggests that, if they could afford it and

find a substitute, they might commute their work for a cash payment. The lone cottage-dweller on the manor had no such duty
to provide work and so may have acted as paid casual labour. The
nine larger tenants paid rent (6s. or 8s.) and worked fewer days for
the landowner, two days harrowing and half a day weeding. They
seem to have commuted their harvest duties at 1s. 6d. each. But
everyone (except the cottager) had to turn out to mow the demesne
meadow, and make two specific payments to the lord each autumn,
at Michaelmas. The two free tenants (as opposed to the others, who
were customary tenants) had no duties except the payment of a
money rent.

By contrast the arrangement on St Mary's manor in 1310 was
much simpler, as all labour services, including those required at
harvest time, appear to have been commuted to money payments.
The manor at this period had eight free and ten customary tenants.

The quality of land varied, and was valued accordingly. At
Ashton Gifford in 1327 about one quarter of the arable was highly
valued, at 8d. or 5d. per acre (the Wiltshire average was 4d.), but
the remainder was regarded as worth only 1d. At St Peter's rather
more than half was worth 4d. or more, but the rest was valued
at 1d. These disparities suggest that the medieval fields had been
extended by breaking up adjacent downland for cultivation, with
disappointing results. A three-field rotation was practised at
Ashton Gifford and St Mary's, and was probably adhered to at St
Peter's also.[76]

From the 16th century onwards sources of information about
Codford's agriculture become more numerous. In June 1552,
wheat, barley, oats, peas, and vetches were all growing in the fields
of Codford St Peter. In subsequent years wheat, barley, and peas

Map 17 Detail of
Codford St Mary Tithe
Award of 1840, showing
field strips.

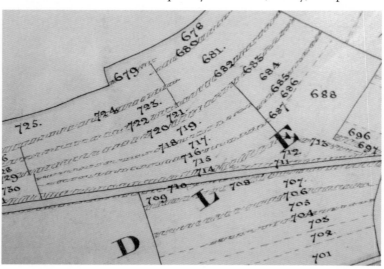

Codford's Domesday Reckoning

Domesday Book, the most famous record in England's national archive, and one of the oldest, has been available in printed form since 1783. Here is a facsimile copy of the original manuscript entry for Codford St Mary, and beneath it the 1783 printed transcript of the same entry, which copies as faithfully as possible the form and abbreviations of the original. There have been four published editions of the Wiltshire portion of Domesday Book since 1783, and two are widely available in libraries, so researchers have no problem in finding out what it records for any Wiltshire community.

If Domesday Book were being compiled today it would take the form of a spreadsheet. Here are the four entries for Codford (1 for Ashton Gifford, 1 for Codford St Mary, 2 for the 2 halves into which Codford St Peter was then divided). Some descriptions and measurements are difficult to interpret; they are discussed below the table.

XXXVII. TERRA WALERAN VENATORIS.

WALERANN ten de rege *COTEFORD*. Erlebald tenuit T.R.E.7 geldb p.vi.hid.Tra.e.vi.car.De ea ft in dnio iii.hide.7 ibi.ii.car.7 iii.ferui.7 vii.uitti 7 vi.bord cu.iii. car.Ibi molin redd.x.fol.7 x.ac pti.Paftura dim leu lg.7 v.qz lat.Valuit x.lib.Modo.xii.lib.

37. LAND OF WALERAN THE HUNTSMAN

Waleran holds Codford [St Mary] of the king. Erlebald held it in the time of King Edward and paid geld for 6 hides. There is land for 6 ploughs. Of this there are in demesne 3 hides and there are 2 ploughs and 3 servi; and there are 7 villani and 6 bordarii with 3 ploughs. There is a mill paying 10 shillings, and 10 acres of meadow. The pasture is one half league long and 5 furlongs broad. It was worth £10; it is now worth £12.

	Ashton	St Mary	St Peter 1	St Peter 2	Total
1086 Owner	Robert	Waleran	Bernard	Osbern	
1066 Owner	Kenwin	Erlebald	-	Aelfric	
Hides	6	6	1.5	1.5	15
Ploughlands	4	6	2	2	14
Demesne hides	3	3	1	1	8
Demesne ploughs	2	2	1	1.5	6.5
Servi	3	3	1	2	9
Villani	4	7	-	-	11
Bordarii	-	6	-	-	6
Cotarii	3	-	2	7	12
Tenants' ploughs	2	3	1	0.5	6.5
Mills	0.5	1	0.25	0.25	2
Mill payment	6s. 3d.	10s.	3s.	3s. 1.5d.	£1 2s. 4.5d.
Meadow	12 acres	10 acres	10 acres	10 acres	42 acres
Pasture	6x6 furlongs	0.5 league x 5 furlongs	4x2 furlongs	4x1 furlong	-
Value 1066	£4	£10	£4	£2.5	£20.5
Value 1086	£6	£12	£3	£3	£24

bordarii: smallholders, lower in status than villani, higher than cotarii

cotarii: cottagers, lower in status than villani or bordarii

demesne: land farmed directly by the landowner

furlongs: linear measurement, one-eighth of a mile

hide: unit of tax assessment based upon the amount of land needed to support one peasant farmer and his household, nominally 120 acres

leagues: linear measurement, perhaps 1.5 miles

ploughland: land to be ploughed by an 8-oxen team, usually equivalent to a hide

servi: unfree employees, in effect slaves, who worked on the demesne

villani: peasant farmers, higher in status than bordarii or cotarii

were the common rotation. The area produced good barley; oats are mentioned only occasionally in inventories. A reference in 1623 to woad suggests that farmers may have been trying to diversify into cash crops, but the evidence of inventories implies that before the 19th century farming remained conservative. The names of the fields begin to be mentioned in documents from the later 16th century, so that it becomes possible to locate the four sets of open fields (see Panel 7). Because Malmpit Hill thrusts southwards almost to the main road, Codford St Mary's farmland was naturally divided into two, with one open-field system on its western slopes facing the village, and a second on the far side.[77]

Terraced strips defined by earth banks known as lynchets on the steeper slopes of the hillside were probably created by extending the fields onto adjacent downland. This would have been taken into cultivation as the population increased between about 1100 and 1300, and later abandoned because of its low yield and low value. Elsewhere in the fields strips were demarcated in various ways, using stones (merestones), stakes or, in St Peter's, turves. Such boundaries were regularly inspected by the tenants, and judgement was passed on anyone accused of moving them for personal gain.[78]

Between 1581 and 1584 Codford St Mary's two sets of open fields were rationalised. This involved agreement in the manorial court between the new lord of the manor, Richard Mompesson, and his freeholders and tenants to a series of land exchanges rationalising the arrangement of holdings according to land-ownership. Three new fields were created, consolidating all the lord's land in one, the freeholders' in a second, and the copy and leaseholders' in a third. From later evidence it seems that the copy and leaseholders' land lay north of the village, the lord's and freeholders' (including richer and more productive soil close to the Wylye) to the east and north-east.[79] Such arrangements do not imply that Mompesson and his freeholders and tenants worked land only in one field, as that would have made the rotation of field use very difficult. Almost certainly the changes simply meant that, while all the land any individual owned or held by copyhold was concentrated in a single field, he or she would be farming in the others as a tenant.

A later innovation, recorded at Codford in 1739, was burn-baking, which involved the paring off, drying and burning of downland turf. The resulting ash spread on the thin chalky soil enriched it with sufficient nutrient to support arable cultivation, at least in the short term. Evidence from Codford fieldnames – Burnbake, Bakeland Field, Old and New Burnt Land – suggests that the practice may have been quite widespread.[80]

The Flock

Although from the Middle Ages both cattle and pigs were kept, sheep were by far the most important livestock in Codford. About 1,400 sheep could be grazed on the downs above the settlement, 800 on St Mary's land, and 200 each on Ashton Gifford, the Giffard estate in St Peter's, and (probably) the other St Peter's estate. The indigenous sheep of the Wylye Valley was the Wiltshire Horn, or Horned Crock, a big-boned large headed sheep with huge spiral horns. Its wool was short and of little value, and the carcass was of only limited worth. The key role of the sheep was in enriching the arable fields, where at the appropriate season the common flocks were brought by night after grazing on the higher downland by day.

From early times sheep brought prosperity to Codford, which in 1332 returned the highest tax assessment of any community in its hundred. The sheep and corn husbandry, essential to maintain the arable land's fertility, made the shepherd a key local figure. One such was Thomas Parsons who died in 1618 leaving 'his shepherd's crook and his scrip' valued at 3d., together with twelve sheep and two sheepskins. His widow Edith died two months later when the crook and scrip were still in the house.[81]

Figure 53 A page from the Codford St Peter Court Book, 1504.

Through its manor courts, Codford's lords and tenants attempted to control the activities of sheep and other animals, to prevent overgrazing and protect the cornland. They regulated with penalties how many and what kind of animals each holding could keep, and where and when they could be depastured. In 1512, for instance, pigs, mares and foals were forbidden to roam on the fields, and in 1516 St Peter's tenants were reported for overloading the landlord's pasture with their sheep. A long-running argument between Codford and Sherrington over shared pasture rights in the Marsh was only finally resolved when the common pasture was inclosed, before 1810, and about eight acres were allotted to Sherrington in compensation for the disputed rights. The problem of straying animals, and of livestock trespassing in Hook Field during the winter, was addressed, after complaints in the 18th century, by providing a pound. In 1810 this pound lay south of the main road near Crouch's Lane. From the frequency of complaints, regulations and punishments we can discern how delicate a balance had to be struck between the needs of livestock and arable farming.[82]

By the 16th century horses were kept for ploughing, together with a few cattle for rearing and the traditional household pig. Animals needed food and grazing rights were jealously guarded. The size of a tenant's holding dictated the number of animals he could pasture. This number was known as his stint, and adjustments to stints led to disputes. For freehold land in Codford St Mary, including the rector's glebe, the sheep stint in 1640 was 50 per yardland. According to glebe terriers it was reduced to 40 and then increased to 45 by 1672. By 1705, however, it was down to 33. The stint for horses and cattle was in dispute. In Codford St Peter the stints seem to have remained static, at 60 sheep, three cattle and three horses per yardland. The only reference to stints in Ashton Gifford, in a lease of 1705, permitted 10 sheep per yardland and mentioned no other livestock.[83]

Details survive from Codford St Peter about the various pastures. Cattle and horses were pastured with the sheep on downland by Chitterne hedge and in the Marsh. In 1624, however, use of the Marsh was restricted to cows, and these had to be overwintered on the manor, thus prohibiting the introduction of heifers from elsewhere for fattening and selling. Among the other common pastures was North Mead, which lay alongside Chitterne Brook; it was a lot-mead, divided among the tenants each year by drawing lots. Even cottagers with little land generally had pasture rights for a cow or two, if not for sheep.[84]

On the downs shade and water for grazing animals were at a premium, and jealously guarded. Chitterne Brook, where it divided Codford St Peter from Chitterne All Saints, was the subject of

an adjudication in 1582 after a dispute between the two manors'
tenants. Thereafter the respective tenants had the right to the green
banks, green ground and land liable to flooding on their own
side of the brook. They could also cross the brook to drive back
straying animals, and animals found on the wrong side were not
impounded, merely driven back. Codford tenants were forbidden
from meddling with four willows belonging to Chitterne in the
marshy ground, and Chitterne tenants could plant four more to
provide shade. There was no source of water for Ashton Gifford
tenants on their downland, which may help to explain why most of
their downs had been converted to arable by the later 18th century.[85]

Enclosure and its Aftermath

Enclosure, whereby the old common fields and pastures were
divided and redistributed to individuals, who thenceforth had
exclusive use of their allotted portion, was a radical and expensive
means of rationalising the use of agricultural land. In Codford
enclosure took place in stages after 1793 and was completed by
1844. Ashton Gifford was first to enclose most of its land, between
1793 and 1806, and its remaining meadow, pasture and downland
in 1815. This was done by private agreement, but the two Codfords

Figure 54 The fields of
the Wylye Valley, showing
the pattern created by
parliamentary enclosure.

The Open Fields

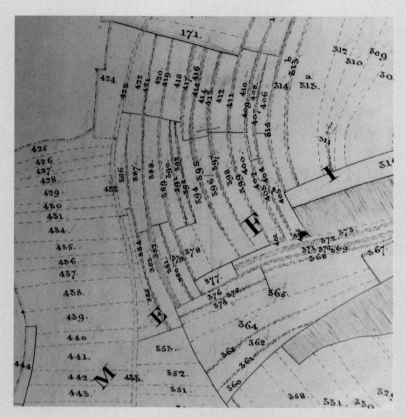

Figure A *Codford St Mary's open fields still existed when its tithe map was drawn in 1840, so the surveyor laboriously plotted every strip. He even shaded in grey the steep banks, known as lynchets, between the curving strips terraced up the hillside. This is part of Home Field, which straddled the Chitterne Road (shown as a dotted line running north-south across the map) north of the village.*

Figure B *Here a similar area (drawn with north orientated to the left) is shown on an estate map of some 80 years earlier. The surveyor names each furlong (Furlong below the Way, Catpill Furlong, Rumsberry Furlong, etc), and shows with dotted lines those holdings made up of 2, 3 or 4 original strips.*

Medieval farming across much of lowland England, including Wiltshire, was a matter less of leafy hedgerows, more of rolling prairies. Arable farming on the Wiltshire chalklands, such as Codford, continued until the 19th century to be organised on the basis of enormous open fields, without hedges or fences, which were divided into blocks of strips (or acres), known as furlongs. Within a furlong all the strips, which were farmed by different owners and tenants, ran in the same direction, often with a slight curve to make turning the plough easier at each end.

Where open field cultivation ended early or was succeeded by permanent grass, for instance, over parts of the Midlands, the former strips often survive

as 'ridge and furrow', but this is rare in Wiltshire. Here the historian must rely on old maps and names in order to reconstruct how the land was farmed. Only on the steeper hillsides, where arable cultivation in strips was more difficult, can be seen strip lynchets, the step-like earthworks which demarcated one strip from the next.

To understand the organisation, extent, and location of a farming community's common fields, and how this affected the development of settlements and farms, a local historian must use maps, documents and surviving place and field names. In Codford there survive an undated 18th-century map of St Mary's, and tithe and enclosure maps from the time in the 19th century when the old system was being abandoned.

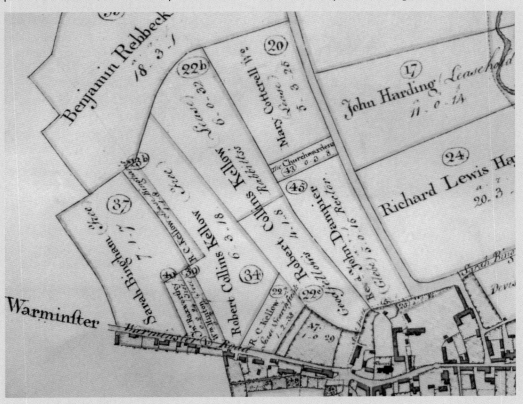

Figure C For Codford St Peter no map of the open field strips survives, but it is still possible to work out where many of them were. This is the enclosure map of 1810 showing an area north and west of St Peter's church. Notice that a few strips remain after most holdings have been consolidated into blocks, and these suggest the direction and length of others that have gone. The jagged boundary at the western edge of the map was clearly drawn round the edges (known as headlands) of the old open field furlongs. In the handwritten award which accompanies this enclosure map many holdings numbered on the map are described with the name of the furlong or field in which the land lay, so the layout of the open field system can be reconstructed.

required local acts of Parliament to achieve enclosure. Arable land in Codford St Peter's fields – Hake, Mead, West Hill, North Mead, Hookland and Braydon Hill – was inclosed in 1810. Consolidated blocks of land were easier to sell, and following enclosure the Earl of Shrewsbury (in 1806) and the earl of Ilchester (in 1812) sold their estates in Ashton Gifford and Codford St Peter respectively.[86]

The delay at Codford St Mary, where enclosure did not take place until 1844, was probably because of opposition from the lord of the manor, Harry Biggs. When the neighbouring parish of Stockton, of which he was also lord, was enclosed in 1815, he seems to have found that the loss of the common sheepfold reduced the fertility and yield of the steeper, thinner arable soils, and he presumably feared a similar outcome in Codford.[87]

Enclosure hastened the demise of old forms of tenure, principally copyhold and fee-farm rents, which might remain fixed for long periods, and so were not sensitive to market forces. They were replaced by short leaseholds and rack rents, which could easily be raised or varied. In St Mary's between 1842 and 1847 copyholders dwindled from five to three and fee-farm renters from seven to five, while rack-rent payers increased from two to nine.[88]

Those dispossessed by enclosure found their wages in Codford as agricultural labourers very low – 'miserable' was how William Cobbett described their condition in 1826. Paupers were forced to work on farms, which kept wages depressed, so that a man's regular weekly income in Ashton Gifford in 1869 was reckoned at 10s., and a woman's 8d. per day. Women, however, only found work at haymaking and harvest, times of peak demand for labour, when a fit man prepared to work up to 15 hours from dawn to dusk might treble his wages. Boys began work at nine years old and earned 1s. 6d. weekly with an extra 6d. for Sunday. This income, some families claimed, was less than it cost to keep a boy at home, but they felt under pressure to send him to work from the farmers who owned their tied cottages.[89]

Sheep and corn husbandry continued to dominate Codford's agriculture. William Bennett's farm in 1830 included 600 sheep but only six cows, and he had five ricks of wheat, three of barley and one of oats. When John Ravenhill let a farm in Codford St Peter to John and William Chisman in 1865 he stipulated that they must keep between 450 and 600 sheep to pen and fold on the arable, and that they were not to plough up grassland without his consent. He, in return, would repair the barn and install a water supply.[90]

The Chismans on another Codford St Peter farm had by 1877 reduced its downland pasture to barely half the arable acreage, and this gradual switch can be seen also at St Mary's. Here, after enclosure in 1844, Harry Biggs leased East Farm to Anthony Notley on

Figure 55 Starveall
Farmstead in 2006. A
little-altered example
of an isolated, mid-
19th-century downland
farmstead.

the understanding that the latter could break up for cultivation 50
acres of downland, and must restore to arable the lynchets within
three years. For his part Biggs would invest in a new complex of
farm buildings close to the Fisherton Delamere boundary, including barns and cattle sheds, a stable and two labourers' cottages, all
within a walled enclosure. These buildings survive and are now
known as Starveall.[91]

From notebooks kept by Notley we learn the scale of his farming. In 1850 he sold sheep worth over £850, and nearly 200 lbs. of
wool. His vast flock at shearing time in 1854 numbered 1,154 ewes
and rams, and 468 lambs had their tails docked. Each year he sent
large numbers of ewes to other farms for feeding. He also kept cows
and pigs, selling piglets to neighbouring farms and sharing his bull
with other Codford farmers. His payments for reaping between
1848 and 1853 ranged from 7s. 6d. to 10s. per acre, the variations
reflecting in part the difficulty of reaping on steep slopes.[92]

Military training, which impacted so heavily on Codford from
1914 and again from 1939, affected farming in two principal ways.
The large military presence offered a market for the products
of dairying and pig farming, thus accelerating the switch from
sheep and corn. But far more significant was the loss of farmland
and access to land resulting from the construction after 1914 of
hutted camps, a military hospital and temporary railway lines.
Affected farmland was not only difficult to sell, but even obtain-
ing compensation from the War Office for the land itself, or for
crops damaged by troop activities such as flying or trench digging,
proved expensive and protracted. And when it was paid, as Manor
Farm's occupant discovered, it covered only about one-third of his
loss. Some commandeered land was not returned until 1924, and
because the foundations of demolished huts were not removed,
their sites could no longer be ploughed.[93]

The Farms in Wartime

In 1941, when wartime Britain was running out of food, the government carried out agricultural surveys (now preserved in The National Archives) with a view to making farming more efficient and productive. Returns to these surveys describe the Codford farms in considerable detail. An example of one of these agricultural land use maps drawn a few years earlier, in about 1936, is shown opposite.

An International 10/20 tractor pulling a binder on Manor Farm c.1945.

EAST FARM (2,850 acres)
650 acres arable, 1,500 acres pasture, 700 acres
   downland.
1,800 sheep, 383 cattle (150 in milk), 101 calves
   for fattening, 38 pigs.
Arable crops: 205 acres mixed corn; 138 acres
   barley; 97 acres wheat; also potatoes and
   fodder crops.
33 farmworkers, including 3 boys, 1 woman, 22
   tied cottages
Since 1940 almost 400 acres of grassland converted to arable.

MANOR FARM (1,062 acres)
501 acres arable, 214 acres permanent grass,
   347 acres rough grazing.
800 sheep (approx.), 79 cows (27 in calf, 1 in
   milk).
Arable crops: 97 acres oats; 90 acres wheat; 87
   acres barley; 5 acres potatoes; also fodder
   crops.
12 farmworkers, including 1 boy, 12 tied cottages (9 let to farmworkers).
Since 1940 about 94 acres of grassland ploughed
   up; some land taken for military use.

MIDDLE FARM (534 acres)
145 acres arable, about 120 acres pasture,
   about 270 acres rough grazing.
92 cattle (26 in milk).
Arable crops: 76 acres barley; 21 acres wheat;
   31 acres oats; 17 acres mixed corn.
7 farmworkers, including 1 boy, 1 woman, 8
   cottages (4 let to service tenancies).
About 74 acres of grassland converted to arable.

MANOR HOUSE FARM (211 acres)
20 acre arable, most of remainder downland or
   rough grazing.
47 cows (45 in-calf heifers).
About 15 acres of grassland converted to
   arable.

SMALLER FARMS:
LOWER FARM (134 acres). All grass dairy farm,
    30 cattle, 18 sheep, 26 pigs, 100 fowls.
BURY FARM (40 acres). Dairy farm, 33 cattle,
    3 goats.
ANZAC FARM (36 acres). Dairy farm, 23 cattle.
MAYFLOWER FARM (34 acres). Grassland, 22
    cattle, 75 pigs, 209 poultry.
CHESTNUTS DAIRY (31 acres). Grassland, 12
    cows, 3 weaners.

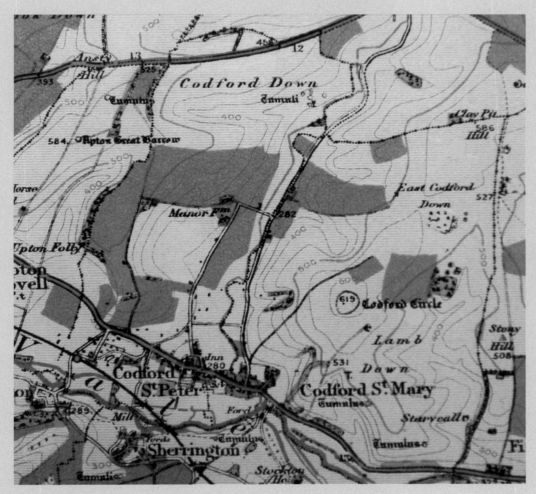

brown = arable
pale green = grassland
dark green = woodland
yellow = rough pasture
purple = buildings, gardens, orchards, paddocks

Figure 56 Manor Farm, Codford in the 1930s showing hay being loaded from the wain onto the elevator.

In 1939 the process was repeated. Virgin sites on farmland were requisitioned for hutted camps, and downland at the Punch Bowl Bottom became a firing range and target area. After the war the camps lingered for several years, and some land was taken for housing rather than returned to agricultural use. Although the economic effects of military occupation in Codford cannot be quantified, it seems that for farming, unlike other sectors of the village economy, they were on the whole detrimental.[94]

A valuable snapshot of farming in Codford in 1941 is provided by a government survey and may be compared with the current position more than sixty years later (see Panel 8). Some farmland has been taken for housing; some, such as Bury and Greenhill Farms, have seen their land go out of agricultural use; and several of the smaller farms have been merged with larger ones. Sheep are

Figure 57 Oxen ploughing on Manor Farm, *c.*1912.

no longer commercially kept in Codford, although a few remain to crop the parkland grass at Ashton Gifford; and the two largest concerns, Manor Farm and East Farm, concentrate on arable and cattle for beef and (at East Farm) dairying. An arable and pig-fattening business continued at Mayflower Farm in 2002; and Auckland Farm's downland was in use for raising young stock from a dairy unit at Upton Lovell.[95]

Woodland

In common with many chalkland communities Codford lacked woodland, a vital commodity for fuel and building, so that use of what little was available was strictly controlled. Leases of 1561 and 1566, for example, stipulated which trees could be cut, and in the 17th century tenants were prohibited from cutting or lopping the few hedgerow elms which were the only trees on the manor. Only for house repairs was permission occasionally given to tenants by the manorial courts to take elms, four times between 1631 and 1637, involving 12 trees in all. Maps from the 18th and 19th centuries suggest that what little woodland existed (31 acres in 1839) lay along the north bank of the Wylye, almost all in Ashton Gifford. Before 1889 in Codford St Mary a conifer plantation was made around Punch Bowl Bottom, and two deciduous plantations, Little Wood and the Belt, on the lower slopes of Malmpit Hill. All these are still there today, as well as small plantations on Manor Farm land, and some magnificent old copper beech trees near St Mary's church and behind the Woolstore.[96]

Map 18 Codford in 1886. Except for a few modern plantations, there was little woodland then.

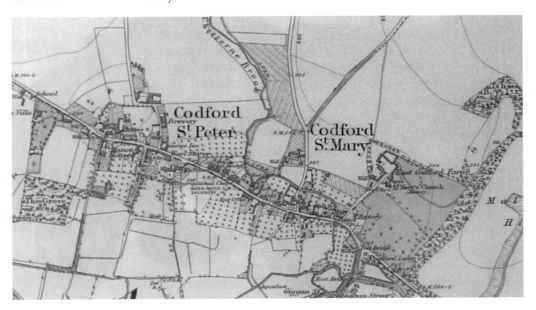

FROM THE RIVER

As well as sustaining life by supplying water for humans and animals to drink, and for domestic hygiene and waste disposal, the River Wylye was an essential component in Codford's economic life. It was the community's power supply and a source of food; it also enabled the farmers, through careful and innovative management, to maximize their stockholding and yields.

Codford's two watermills recorded in Domesday Book are poorly documented. The mill belonging to St Mary's manor had an annual value of 20s. in 1349, and may then have been used for fulling cloth as well as, or instead of, grinding corn. It probably occupied the site of a 19th-century mill, converted to a dwelling house by 1839, which stood south of the river but north of the parish boundary, on Giggan Street. The site of the other Domesday mill, serving the three estates which made up Codford St Peter and Ashton Gifford, is unknown, but it too may have been a fulling mill in the 14th century. After 1400 and in 1645 Ashton Gifford was said to have possessed two mills, but there is no later record of them, and they may have stopped working when water meadow works upstream affected river flows and levels. Sherrington mill, just south of the parish boundary, would have provided an easily accessible alternative for Codford farmers.[97]

The right to take fish from the Wylye was (and is) a valuable economic asset, jealously guarded by its possessors and scrupulously recorded in documents. Indeed this activity gave Codford's western neighbour, Fisherton Delamere, the first element of its name. After Lord Giffard's possessions were confiscated by the Crown in 1322 his Ashton Gifford fishery was leased and fish with an annual value of 13s. 4d. were sold. In 1581 an Ashton Gifford resident pleaded not guilty to infringing fishing rights, and in 1623 another fishing dispute resulted in a lawsuit. Fishing rights

Figure 58 The junction of High Street and Chitterne Road, flooded during the First World War.

Figure 59 Codford's water meadows were visible as parch marks during the hot, dry summer of 1976.

A mile above the town ... the stream divides itself into many streamlets, and there is a district called the Water Meads, in which bridges are more frequent than trustworthy, in which there are hundreds of little sluicegates for regulating the irrigation.

From *The Vicar of Bullhampton* by Anthony Trollope, first published in 1870.

continued to be conveyed with the title to Codford estates in the 1920s, but because of their sporting value they have subsequently been sold separately.[98]

Floated water meadows, which are so characteristic a feature of south Wiltshire's river valleys, were an innovation of the early 17th century (see Panel 9) and there are references suggesting that the practice came very early to Codford. John Topp constructed a weir in Codford St Mary in about 1621; in 1633 Thomas Lambert built hatches and had land covered by water; and in 1656 part of the river was straightened. But irrefutable evidence of water meadows only comes much later, when Thomas Alford was paid in 1795 to repair existing hatches, make new hatches, and convert a withy bed into 'good water meadow'. By 1839 almost all Codford's low-lying land close to the Wylye, 154 acres, was described as water meadow, and soon afterwards meadows beside the Chitterne Brook were floated as well. Although some of Codford's water meadows were still used in the mid-20th century, most had been ploughed up or reverted to conventional, if marshy, meadow and pasture.[99]

THE ENTREPRENEURS

Until 1914 agriculture dominated Codford's economy. Such trading as took place depended on a by-product of the prevailing sheep and corn husbandry – wool – or was passing trade, catering to the needs of travellers along the valley road.

In 1254 the Crown granted the lord of Codford St Mary a charter permitting him to hold a weekly market. This may have been

Floated Water Meadows

Everyone who travels around the chalkland areas of Wiltshire, Hampshire and Dorset will have noticed the corrugated pattern of ridges and ditches in the meadows beside the principal rivers. They are the remains of floated water meadows, an innovation of the 17th century which aimed to encourage a lusher and earlier growth of meadow grass each spring. This was achieved by creating a slow but steady flow of river water right across the meadow (known as 'drowning' the meadow), thus keeping the ground slightly warmer than it would be if exposed to winter frosts, and also nourishing it with alluvial deposits. The earlier and better the grass, the more sheep could be kept through the winter. More sheep resulted in more manure, and more manure resulted in better crop yields.

Creating a floated water meadow was expensive and involved skilful surveying and engineering. A main carriage (rather like a mill leat) was created, drawing water from the river upstream of the meadow. The intake and flow along it were controlled by hatches – small removable wooden dams. When full to overflowing the main carriage spilled water into smaller channels, known as carriers, which fanned out across the meadow. Between the carriers, and slightly lower, were drains, which fed the water into a main or tail drain, which in turn took the water back to the river further downstream. The operation was controlled by a drowner, who regulated the hatches and carriers to adjust the flow.

A few floated meadows can still be worked, and many more disused systems can still be seen such as at Britford in Wiltshire, shown here. Even where they have largely disappeared, as in Codford, evidence that they existed can be found on maps. The diagram shows part of a surviving meadow on the River Avon at Lower Woodford near Salisbury (from Michael Cowan's book, *Wiltshire Water Meadows*, Salisbury: Hobnob Press 2005).

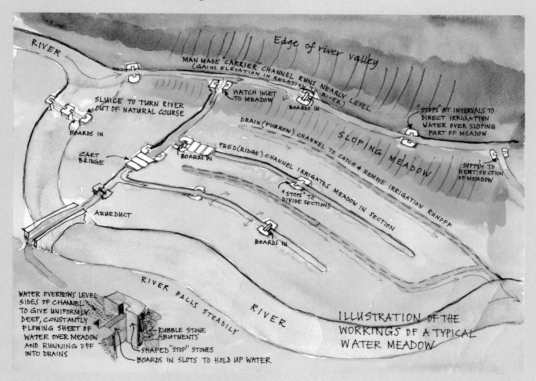

Figure A *Illustration of the working of a typical water meadow.*

Figure B *A few floated meadows can still be worked, and many more disused systems can still be seen such as at Britford in Wiltshire, shown here.*

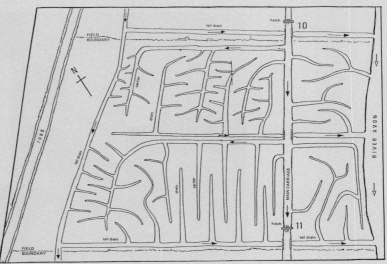

Figure C *Diagram of part of surviving water meadow on the River Avon at Lower Woodford.*

Figure 60 Watercolour of 1892, showing Codford St Peter High Street and the location of the original *George Inn*.

ratification of a market already being held without permission, it may have been a genuinely new market, or the grant may have been obtained merely as a status symbol, with no real intention of being acted upon. In any case Codford's proximity to the fledgling town of Heytesbury and the much more vigorous market centre of Warminster would all have conspired to defeat any marketing experiment. Indeed, the only suggestion that Codford might ever have held a market is the lane called Cheapside – 'cheap' derives from a word for market.[100]

Innkeeping stood a better chance of success, and evidence for it at Codford St Peter is first encountered in 1516, when nine tenants were engaged in brewing and one was a hosteller selling provisions. The *George Inn*, first recorded in 1541–2, had become the stopping-place for the *Rocket* stagecoach before 1800, and was described in 1787 as a stone and timber thatched building, whose landlord operated two post-chaises. It was rebuilt in brick in 1893 slightly further from the road, and survives as the only public house in Codford. Other licensed premises included the *King's Arms*, which stood south of the main road near the Hindon Lane junction and was demolished around the 1890s; the *New Inn* at Codford St Peter, mentioned in the 1780s; and a Victorian beerhouse, the *Fleur-de-Lys*, which stood at French Horn. The *King's Arms* had been in existence since the mid-18th century, and towards the end of its life the retired butler and his wife who ran it were offering accommodation to trout fishermen.[101]

Codford St Peter had a tobacconist in 1637 (probably one of its innkeepers), and in the 19th century a number of shopkeepers, a baker, smithy and two carriers. During the 1850s and 1860s there were racehorse stables, and trainers occur in St Peter's registers

Figure 61 The *George Inn* after it had been rebuilt further back on the site.

in 1856 and 1861. A racecourse was marked out on East Codford Down after 1900.

Wool Sorting

Codford's principal industry derived from its numerous sheep. Four weavers left probate inventories between 1550 and 1740, and a domestic spinning industry also existed. The Topp family who bought much of Codford St Mary from Giles Mompesson in the early 17th century had built their grand manor house at Stockton a generation earlier on the profits of clothmaking. But only in the 19th century did wool sorting and stapling become important to Codford's economy, and this industry has left the village its most idiosyncratic complex of buildings, the Woolstore and its associated structures.[102]

The fleece of the local Wiltshire Horn was almost non-existent. It resembled a coat of hair rather than a woolly fleece, and indeed the ewes were almost bare on their bellies. The wool which they produced was probably used in the carpet trade, which developed at Wilton, further east along the valley. For cloth production, fleeces were imported, either from elsewhere in Wiltshire, or, quite commonly, from Spain. But whatever the uses to be found for them, the fleeces were selected and purchased by a wool stapler, often in the field before shearing, and taken to his wool store to be sorted and graded before being sold on to the cloth trade. In the case of Codford, sorted wool would be sent to mills along the Wylye Valley, the most likely being that at Upton Lovell, where the wool would be cleaned and scoured to remove dirt, natural grease and impurities. The wool would then have been blended to form a uniform yarn and carded to tease out the staple fibres prior to weaving.[103]

Wool sorting was the best-paid process in the whole woollen industry. It involved the separation, sorting and grading of the different fleeces and different parts of the fleece and relied very much on feel and intuition. The sorters would sit or stand at a long, lighted bench, with slats in it to let through the dust and other debris. Behind each sorter would be large barrels or baskets, into which they would put the sorted wool. However, until the 19th century wool sorting could be a hazardous business, since imported fleeces, such as mohair, camel hair and cashmere, could carry a human form of anthrax. No masks were worn to eliminate dust and it seems unlikely that the windows were opened very often, if at all. The only benefit from the handling of raw wool was the lanolin which would be present in great quantities and which is normally used to soften the skin. But even this may have become distasteful to the workers after a time.

Figure 62 A Wiltshire Horn sheep. This slender, long-legged breed is indigenous to the Codford area and ideally suited to the steep downs.

At Codford, the Woolstore, where fleeces were kept for collection by a dealer, together with the owner's mansion house, were almost certainly built in the early 1820s for James Raxworthy, a member of a family which had originated in Somerset but by the mid-18th century had established itself at Boyton on the south bank of the Wylye. From here they spread to Heytesbury and Upton Lovell, where they may have had an interest in the mill. By 1773 they had property in Codford; the Land Tax assessment returns for Ashton Gifford record a 'Mr Raxworthy' in 1773, paying 16s. 6d. tax. He presumably was the John Raxworthy who from 1780 onwards was the owner of land or property, let out to John Polden from 1780 onwards and to John Foley from 1798 to 1806, and in his own occupation from 1817 until 1831, when the records cease. By 1815 Raxworthy was recorded as having some 26 acres in the area.

John Raxworthy and his wife Dyonisia lived in Upton Lovell where they raised a family of eight children between 1787 and 1800. John died in 1835 and his son James, by then forty-two, inherited. James Raxworthy was baptised in 1793 and in 1822 married his second cousin, Dyonisia Barnes, who had been born in Collingbourne Kingston. Her father was a gentleman and there is some indication that the family may have been connected with the Stock Exchange and the East India Company. Perhaps it was at about the time of their marriage that the Woolstore building, as we now know it, was built. Certainly the Wool House mansion dates from around this time.[104] (See Chapter 2.)

Neither James nor his father made any reference to the wool business in their wills. Both recorded themselves as 'gentleman' and the family seems to have been quite wealthy; certainly the children were all well-provided for. Nevertheless, in the census returns of 1841 the term wool stapler (referring to the man who bought the fleeces) was used of James Raxworthy and one other, Leonard Barns, probably James's foreman.

James himself died in 1856. Although his son, also James, who had started his working life in wool sorting, retained ownership of the Woolstore until 1871, he seems to have given up running the

Figure 63 Wool sorting in the Woolstore in the late 19th century.

business. Recorded as an agent for artificial manure, in the census returns of 1871, he was perhaps a participant in the '*guano-rush*'. At all events by the time of the next census, in 1881, the Raxworthy's connexion with the Woolstore had ceased. George Dear had taken over both it and the adjacent mansion.[105]

George Sedley Dear, who came from Durnford in the Woodford Valley, north of Salisbury, seems to have purchased the estate in 1872 from a certain Edward Atkinson, and lived at the house with his wife, Emma, his eight children, two nurses and two servants. Between about 1876 and 1885 he also took over the woollen mill at Upton Lovell. By 1882 he had enlarged the loom sheds and fitted a new steam engine, and the business was thriving. In 1886, however, he sold it to William Walker, when it became the Upton Lovell Manufacturing Company. In 1899 the mill was damaged by fire and the cloth trade in the upper Wylye Valley virtually came to an end.[106]

Although, under the terms of Dear's will, the wool-sorting business in Codford was to be offered for sale to each of his sons in turn, after his death in 1899, his wife seems to have taken charge. Emma is recorded as a wool merchant in 1901 when her son Alec was manager of the Woolstore and another relative, William Dear, was foreman. The business was still under George's name in the local directories until 1907, the year before Emma died. In 1907 Giles Conduit, a Codford man, took over from William Dear as foreman. From 1911 until 1923 George's son Alec is listed in the local directories as 'woolstapler', after which date they make no further reference to the business. The electoral rolls for Codford, however, continue to list Alec Dear as manager of the Woolstore, living in the mansion house, called The Beeches, until 1926, when he moved to Moortown, Ringwood, in Hampshire.[107]

There are no known surviving employment records, so the only indications of who worked at the Woolstore as wool sorters grading the fleeces are to be found in the 19th-century census returns. The Woolstore staff seem to have averaged about nine during the second half of the century. In 1841 there were nine known wool sorters, six in Codford St Peter and three in Codford St Mary, as well as the two wool staplers already mentioned. It is, however, sometimes difficult to work out the nature and size of the workforce since the terms stapler and sorter could be used interchangeably. By 1851, James Raxworthy was recorded as a wool stapler employing twelve men. Two of these were his sons, James and John, three were from Codford St Peter and three from Codford St Mary. All these are listed as wool staplers and a further three wool sorters were living in Codford St Peter. Some workers may have been drawn from other nearby villages and an examination of the census returns for these might reveal other wool sorters in the area. Only Corton has been looked at so far. The figures found for likely workers at the Woolstore are as follows:

1841   2 wool staplers, 9 wool sorters
1851   9 wool staplers, 3 wool sorters, 1 wool sorter from Corton
1861   5 wool staplers, 6 wool sorters
1871   2 wool staplers, 3 wool sorters
1881   2 wool staplers, 2 wool sorters, 2 apprentices,
          4 unemployed wool sorters
1891   2 wool staplers, 7 wool sorters, 1 wool sorter from Corton
1901   1 merchant (the manager's mother), 1 manager, 4 wool
          staplers (one an assistant to his father), 1 wool sorter.[108]

In 1871, wool sorting in Codford seems to have been at an all-time low and James Raxworthy the younger had evidently given up the business. The slump and the departure of Raxworthy may have been due to expenses incurred in a Chancery case, which had caused the whole estate to be put up for auction just two or three years earlier. As it turned out, the business was saved, though it is not known how, since a number of lots were withdrawn on the day of the auction, including the main sites of the Woolstore and mansion house. [109]

By 1881 the situation had hardly improved. Out of nine men connected with the business, two were apprentices and four were unemployed. Together with the two wool staplers, George Dear, the owner, and William Dear, his foreman, the work force in Codford comprised two apprentices and two wool sorters. Whether other wool sorters were employed from surrounding villages is not known.

Figure 64 The Woolstore staff, *c.*1898. The carter stands to the left, with his whip.

Figure 65 Stokes
Stores on the north
side of the High Street,
photographed in 1914.

In the staff photograph, taken in the late 1890s, there appear to be fifteen staff, plus two gentlemen 'in charge' and a carter. Eight of the men wore white coats beneath aprons – perhaps these were the actual wool sorters at the time and the rest were auxiliary staff, employed in the office. At least one of the suited gentlemen is believed to have been a member of the Dear family.[110]

NEW SHOPS AND SERVICES

The First World War transformed Codford's trading and employment potential. Three banks, two cinemas and a veterinary hospital had opened in the village by 1915, and shops and other services were provided in houses, gardens and temporary buildings constructed along the main road. They included a chemist, a barber, an ironmonger and a tobacconist. Although this bonanza was short-lived, some businesses remained after 1918, as Codford adapted to being a roadside village along an increasingly busy thoroughfare. One shop became a petrol station by 1920, was enlarged a decade later, and continued to trade until 1973, the premises subsequently being used by a motor-caravan business. Between the wars businesses opening in Codford included a hairdresser, a bicycle workshop, a corn merchant (in premises near Codford railway station later used as a plastics factory), a laundry and a transport café (the Hillside Café, near the western parish boundary, which still caters for passing traffic).[111]

Figure 66 Shops on the
north side of the High
Street during the First
World War.

Figure 67 The Milk
Bar on the corner of
Chitterne Road and the
High Street in the 1930s.

The soldiers returned in 1939 and with them the economic
boom. Wages rose, more jobs were available, and some businesses
prospered, such as the milk bar which had opened in a somewhat
vulnerable position (considering the heavy military manoeuvring)
on the corner of Chitterne Road the previous year. After the war
passing trade increased as travel became easier, and at first this
was to Codford's benefit. In 1964 the village boasted seven food
shops and six other retailers, as well as visiting mobile tradesmen
and banks. But by 1974, when the milk bar was demolished, the
number of shops had fallen to ten, and by 1989 only five remained,
including one antiques shop. After the bypass opened the tally fell
to three, where it remains – a general store and post office forming part of the New Road petrol station, the antiques shop, and a
specialist farm food shop at East Farm.[112]

Against this background other businesses have opened,
including a seafood importer on an isolated site off Chitterne
Road; a Little Chef restaurant and a pony trekking centre, both
close to the Hillside Café in the west of the parish; and the head-
quarters of the Country Gentlemen's Association on the site of the
former railway station.

Figure 68 Doughty House
on the south side of the
High Street in 1914. Mr
and Mrs Payne ran a
religious bookshop from
their house there.

Chapter 5

Friends and Neighbours

THE ORDERING OF SOCIETY

The Village Elite

Before 1800, as we saw in Chapter 3, none of Codford's manorial owners ever lived in the village. Although there was no resident lord, the house in Codford St Peter called the Manor House was from time to time the residence of the manorial steward. It is to be distinguished from the Old Manor House which was probably the home of the tenant responsible for the demesne (home) farm. In St Mary's the present East Codford Farm was the demesne farm, and there was another substantial farmhouse at Ashton Gifford, recorded in the 16th century, which may have occupied the site of the present house.[113]

Because the principal farms were leased in the Middle Ages, those lessees whose families resided and persisted in the village may have come to be regarded as the leaders of local society. Robert le Bor, for instance, amassed leasehold land in both Codfords and Ashton Gifford between 1305 and 1321, some of which he sublet. In 1338 his estate (or part of it) was sold to the Balle family, who retained it until 1419, and then sold it to Thomas Tropnell. He bought other land in both parishes and the estate remained in his family until 1548, although it is unlikely that any of them resided in Codford.[114]

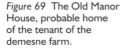

Figure 69 The Old Manor House, probable home of the tenant of the demesne farm.

After the Middle Ages, as we have seen, lessees were more
transient. At East Farm the lease of Edward Slade, lessee in 1561,
was renewed for 18 years in 1568, but in 1588 there was a different
lessee, who sublet portions of the estate. In the 18th century a lease
was reduced from 16 to eight years. The Ashton Gifford demesne
was leased in 1485–6, and in 1566 its farmhouse was reported to
be out of repair, either through standing empty or because of its
lessee's neglect. John Turner, a lessee in the 1630s, was clearly struggling, as he accumulated a debt to the lord of over £5 in two years.
The Codford St Peter demesne was leased to John Prior in 1582,
who had to provide a gelding for the lord's occasional use when he
visited, and in 1595 to John Bright, whose heirs sublet it in 1634.[115]

After 1800 the role of benevolent squire was taken by William
Hubbard and his successors. Hubbard built Ashton Gifford House
and retained the estate until 1836. Wadham Locke, his successor,
built Ashton Gifford school in 1844, and John Ravenhill, who
bought the estate in 1850, continued his interest in the school,
served as first chairman of the Warminster Board of Guardians and
engaged in other judicial and philanthropic activities. Codford St
Mary also had a Victorian lord of the manor, Harry Biggs, who, if
not actually resident, lived nearby at Stockton House.[116]

Beneath the squires in Victorian society were the gentleman
farmers. William Bennett, a substantial Codford landowner and
lessee, owned two fancy carriages – a miniature brougham and
a park phaeton. Like Anthony Notley, lessee of East Farm, he
served as a poor law guardian, and Anthony's son Charles was
elected a district councillor in 1895. Other leaders of Codford

Figure 71 East (or East Codford) Farm, in the early 20th century, probably originally the demesne farm of the manor of Codford St Mary and later the home of the lessee.

society, though not aspiring to the status of gentlemen, would have included Thomas Slade Whiting, the major farmer and landowner in Codford St Peter, and Robert Raxworthy, owner of the Woolstore.[117]

Tenants, Peasants and Farmhands

Most of the Codford households listed in Domesday Book, apart from those of the servants on the demesnes, seem to have possessed a little land, perhaps a nominal 12 or 24 acres. But as the population nationally increased over the next two centuries, so did the inequalities. At Codford around 1300 two tenants had increased their holdings to around 50 acres each, at the expense of seven, who had little or no land at all. Another 32 still fell into the 12 to 24 acres bracket, and an unknown number were tenants of one of the Codford St Peter manors, for which no data exist. A snapshot of most Codford tenants, with their names, is provided by a tax return in 1332, although the poorest were exempt and there may have been some evasion. The clearest trend to emerge is that the 14 Ashton Gifford tenants, though fewer in number, were rather more prosperous, typically paying between 2s. and 3s. tax, whereas most of the 44 Codford tenants paid between 8d. and 2s.[118]

Between 1582 and 1776 a series of manorial surveys exists for Codford St Peter, and these give a good impression of the changing social status and wealth of the peasantry. Throughout this period there were two holdings of three yardlands (about 75 acres) and between six and eight holdings of one half or one yardland (12–24 acres). Thus among the tenantry with small landholdings there was relative stability. It was among the peasants who occupied cottages and tenements with little or no land attached, often built on manorial waste, that the greatest change is seen. In 1582 there were 10 such cottages, including three newly-built, and still 10 in 1623, but about 19 by 1776. These landless cottagers, in order to survive, must have been employed as labourers by their fellow villagers, or earned a living from other, non-agricultural, activities.[119]

No doubt William Cobbett's remark, made when he rode through Codford in 1826, that, 'it is not very easy for the eyes of man to discover labouring people more miserable' had such cottagers in mind. Farm labourers with only a small patch of land, or none at all, had to supplement the family income by trade and seasonal work, and they fluctuated between breadline self-sufficiency and parish poor relief. From a low point of 8s. per week in the 1830s the adult wage had only risen to 10s. by 1869, with work for women and overtime for men only available at haymaking and harvest, or when special tasks, such as the back-breaking turnip-hoeing, had to be done.[120]

Subsequently agricultural wages did improve, and such workers continued to form a substantial class in Codford society until after 1914. But the availability of farm work was steadily diminishing, so that by the 1940s there can only have been farm work for around 60 to 65 out of a male population approaching four hundred. By the later 20th century, as the local farms became larger and highly mechanized, agricultural workers as a social group had almost disappeared from the parish.[121]

RUNNING THINGS

In Codford as elsewhere until parish councils were established in 1894 ultimate responsibility for grass-roots local government in England rested with local landowners and the church. In practice, however, much of the day-to-day running of parish affairs depended upon local men of good standing who acted as suitors in the manorial courts or participated in church affairs as church-wardens or later as the members of the parish meetings known as vestries. Because there were several manors in Codford, and two parishes, the community's government has been fragmented, and the survival of records is poor and haphazard (see Chapter 3).

A further complication is the persistence through the Middle Ages of an older framework of local government, akin to self-regulation or community policing, based on units known as tithings and hundreds. When the system was formalised in late

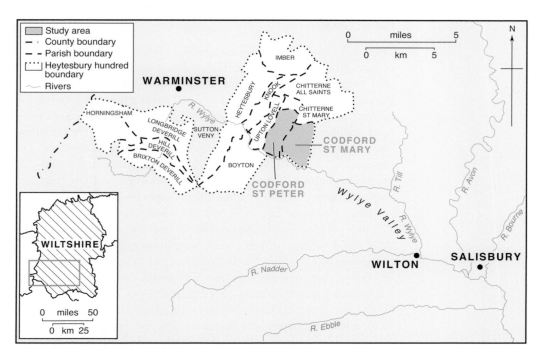

Map 19 Map of the hundred of Heytesbury. One of the administrative units into which Wiltshire was divided from Anglo-Saxon times and which included the two Codford parishes.

Anglo-Saxon England, groupings of ten households (tithings) reported to groupings of ten tithings (hundreds), which reported in turn to the shire or Crown officers. Such decimal precision soon disappeared but the structure remained, so that Ashton Gifford and both Codfords were regarded as tithings, and each formed parts of the hundred of Heytesbury. Attendance was required at quarterly hundred courts, and the tithings were represented by designated tithingmen or other tenants, who stood surety for the good behaviour of the tithing generally (this was known as the view of frankpledge), and reported any problems or misdemeanours.

Thus in 1245–6 Ashton Gifford's tithingman attended four sessions of the hundred court, accompanied in November and at Easter by two tenants. Much later, in the early 16th century, Ashton Gifford was sometimes represented by four men, but their attendance was erratic. The Codford tenants at this period made payments to the lord of Heytesbury hundred, to guarantee that they would hold manorial courts (cert money), or to excuse them from attending. They also reported minor offences, such as incorrect brewing, playing at dice and other illegal games, including one called 'boles', and finding ownerless stray animals. [122]

Parish Government

Codford's two parishes, like everywhere else, had an assortment
of local government responsibilities thrust upon them from the
mid-16th century, but little information about their activities
has survived until much later. Principal among the duties of the
vestries, as parish meetings were known, was the supervision of
road maintenance and poor relief. In the 17th century the parishes
were not very effective at maintaining either the main road or
the road to Chitterne, and they were frequently reported to the
overseeing county authority, the quarter sessions. In 1616, the
men of Codford St Mary excused themselves by explaining that
roadmending stone had to be brought a long way, from Chilmark.
The two parish officials responsible for overseeing repairs to St
Peter's and Ashton Gifford's roads were known in the mid-19th
century as waywardens. Their annual accounts were presented for
inspection, but have not survived. The parish continued to appoint
a waywarden until the early 20th century.[123]

The first recorded vestry business in Codford St Mary's parish, in
1776, related to a charitable donation. The distribution of charities
was one of the responsibilities of the poor overseers, and in Codford
St Mary's – unusually – service as overseer seems to have been an
obligation attached to particular tenements. One tenant chosen on
this basis in the later 19th century objected, on the grounds that
he was a working man with no time to undertake the duties, and
no money to employ someone else to do them. In the 1830s the
St Peter's overseers offset the cost of distributing money, food and
other supplies, medical treatment and funerals, by setting poor men
to work on the roads. Other paupers worked on the overseers' own
farms, including one woman who was taken from the workhouse in
the later 19th century and employed, perhaps as a housemaid.[124]

Codford St Peter's vestry in the years around 1900 met at Easter,
and appointed not only the waywarden and poor overseer (whose
duties until 1925 included valuing property and collecting poor
rates), but also a poor law guardian (to represent the parish on
workhouse business), sometimes a sexton and occasionally a parish
clerk. Between 1857 and 1863 the rector chaired the meetings, but
thereafter until 1914 there was always a lay chairman. A core of
about six people rotated the offices, often in plurality and usually
for several years; frequently only three or four members of the
vestry attended meetings.[125]

By the later 19th century, as various local government functions were taken over by other bodies, most vestry business was
concerned with the church and religious life of the parish. This
included in both parishes the appointment of churchwardens – one

chosen by the rector, one elected by the vestry – and the approval of
their accounts. By 1925, when the first surviving records of Codford
St Mary's parish vestry occur, the meeting was held at Easter in St
Mary's school, and doubled as the parochial church council. The
rector chaired both meetings and membership was almost identi-
cal. In St Peter's the parochial church council met twice each spring,
first at the rectory to update the electoral roll, and then at a second
meeting in the church. Here the roll was approved and churchwardens and council members were elected. Additionally in St
Mary's parish the council appointed sidesmen, approved charities'
accounts, and received a report from the rector on church attendance. Both parishes continued to hold separate parochial church
council meetings after they were formally united in 1930.[126]

The Civil Parishes

Legislation in 1894 created the system of parish councils (in
parishes of over 300 population) and parish meetings (under 300).
Codford St Mary was large enough to qualify for a council, but St
Peter's was not, and had to be content with a meeting. Each parish
elected a councillor to serve on the next tier of local government,
Warminster Rural District Council. First suggested in 1919, in 1934
the two parishes were amalgamated, and thereafter one parish
council has served the whole Codford community. Also in 1934
the rural district in which Codford lay was enlarged, to become
Warminster and Westbury RDC; this tier was further enlarged and

Figure 73 This attractive roundel includes a device of two linked letters W for Warminster and Westbury Rural District Council, which was responsible for the construction of these houses in The Grove.

its functions altered in 1974, with the creation of West Wiltshire District Council.

Seven parishioners (from 14 nominated) were elected to Codford St Mary's Parish Council by a meeting of about 50 electors in December 1894. Thomas Chisman was the first chairman, and Charles Notley of East Farm the first treasurer. At least one meeting was held each year, in the spring, when councillors and officers were elected or appointed. Meetings were held in the schoolroom and, as well as routine business such as approving charity accounts, matters of special concern included housing and the condition of roads, bridges, stiles and footpaths. A joint meeting to discuss housing was held with Codford St Peter in 1919. In the same year the St Peter's parish meeting, which had been held since 1894 (initially under the rector's chairmanship), petitioned to be given parish council powers, but the request was refused because of its small population.[127]

Codford's representation on the rural district council settled down by an 'unwritten law' to one Conservative and one Liberal councillor – one church, one chapel. According to the rector of St Mary's in 1909 there was a certain amount of political 'feeling' between their respective congregations at election time. Much more acrimonious was the first election of a district councillor for St Mary's in 1894. Charles Notley, the principal farmer in the parish, assumed that he would be elected unopposed, but was challenged by a candidate from the newly formed Labour party, an Upton Lovell spinner named George Hinton. The two men tied, and the stalemate was eventually resolved in Notley's favour. One of Notley's supporters printed anonymously a squib in verse, which described Hinton as 'a rank outsider and meddlesome busybody', implied that he was ill-educated and denigrated his followers as 'Lazarites' (lepers).[128]

In March 1934 seven councillors, including the rector, were elected to form the parish council of the united parish. The annual spring meeting was supplemented by others called for particular business, and after 1948 they were held in the YMCA hut, which was later the Codford Club. The acquisition of the hut for the parish, and land for playing fields at Broadleaze, were among the council's concerns, as well as rubbish removal, housing and policing. But for many years the danger and damage caused by increasing traffic along the main road was the main preoccupation, and the council participated in the decision-making processes which finally agreed the route of the bypass.[129]

Figure 74 Codford Club. Once used by First World War troops, and later by the British Legion, it was bought for the parish in 1947 and demolished to make way for the housing (Broadleaze) which paid for its replacement, the modern village hall.

SERVING THE COMMUNITY

Charities

Acts of generosity, kindness and support generally go unrecorded, and indeed it is in the spirit of helping and giving that this should be so. Any historian's attempt to delve into a community's compassion, therefore, is bound to fail, and the people of Codford have been commendably reticent about such matters. What little evidence survives relates to charitable bequests and the statutory provision for the poor at parish level.

The oldest parish charity relevant to Codford is Stockton Almshouse, to which Codford St Mary parishioners have an equal right of entry with those of Stockton, their neighbours across the river. Founded in the mid-17th century, it provided in 1714 for housing, fuel, clothing and a weekly allowance for eight elderly poor. Thus amply provided for, many inmates lived to a great age. Applicants in 2002, as well as satisfying the residential qualification, had to be over 60 and of good character.[130]

Eleven charities for the poor specific to the Codford parishes are known, but three have long been lost. Five of the others related to St Peter's, where poverty was greater, and three to St Mary's. None was earlier than 1776. In order to qualify for the money or coal on offer, recipients had to be elderly, widowed or orphaned, and morally sound in the judgement of the parish officials. All such charities were included in an official report published in 1908, when such doles may have been significant, but by 2002 those that survived had been amalgamated, and their meagre largesse was distributed each Christmas to about twelve elderly residents of the united parish.[131]

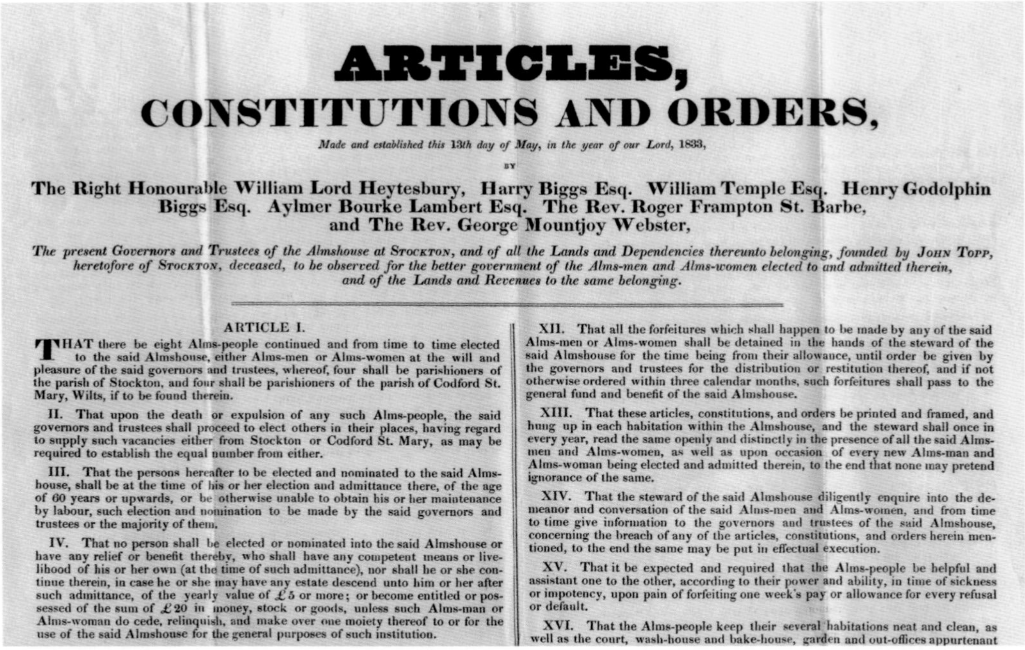

ARTICLES,
CONSTITUTIONS AND ORDERS,

Made and established this 13th day of May, in the year of our Lord, 1833,

BY

The Right Honourable William Lord Heytesbury, Harry Biggs Esq. William Temple Esq. Henry Godolphin Biggs Esq. Aylmer Bourke Lambert Esq. The Rev. Roger Frampton St. Barbe, and The Rev. George Mountjoy Webster,

The present Governors and Trustees of the Almshouse at Stockton, and of all the Lands and Dependencies thereunto belonging, founded by John Topp, heretofore of Stockton, deceased, to be observed for the better government of the Alms-men and Alms-women elected to and admitted therein, and of the Lands and Revenues to the same belonging.

ARTICLE I.

THAT there be eight Alms-people continued and from time to time elected to the said Almshouse, either Alms-men or Alms-women at the will and pleasure of the said governors and trustees, whereof, four shall be parishioners of the parish of Stockton, and four shall be parishioners of the parish of Codford St. Mary, Wilts, if to be found therein.

II. That upon the death or expulsion of any such Alms-people, the said governors and trustees shall proceed to elect others in their places, having regard to supply such vacancies either from Stockton or Codford St. Mary, as may be required to establish the equal number from either.

III. That the persons hereafter to be elected and nominated to the said Almshouse, shall be at the time of his or her election and admittance there, of the age of 60 years or upwards, or be otherwise unable to obtain his or her maintenance by labour, such election and nomination to be made by the said governors and trustees or the majority of them.

IV. That no person shall be elected or nominated into the said Almshouse or have any relief or benefit thereby, who shall have any competent means or livelihood of his or her own (at the time of such admittance), nor shall he or she continue therein, in case he or she may have any estate descend unto him or her after such admittance, of the yearly value of £5 or more; or become entitled or possessed of the sum of £20 in money, stock or goods, unless such Alms-man or Alms-woman do cede, relinquish, and make over one moiety thereof to or for the use of the said Almshouse for the general purposes of such institution.

XII. That all the forfeitures which shall happen to be made by any of the said Alms-men or Alms-women shall be detained in the hands of the steward of the said Almshouse for the time being from their allowance, until order be given by the governors and trustees for the distribution or restitution thereof, and if not otherwise ordered within three calendar months, such forfeitures shall pass to the general fund and benefit of the said Almshouse.

XIII. That these articles, constitutions, and orders be printed and framed, and hung up in each habitation within the Almshouse, and the steward shall once in every year, read the same openly and distinctly in the presence of all the said Alms-men and Alms-women, as well as upon occasion of every new Alms-man and Alms-woman being elected and admitted therein, to the end that none may pretend ignorance of the same.

XIV. That the steward of the said Almshouse diligently enquire into the demeanor and conversation of the said Alms-men and Alms-women, and from time to time give information to the governors and trustees of the said Almshouse, concerning the breach of any of the articles, constitutions, and orders herein mentioned, to the end the same may be put in effectual execution.

XV. That it be expected and required that the Alms-people be helpful and assistant one to the other, according to their power and ability, in time of sickness or impotency, upon pain of forfeiting one week's pay or allowance for every refusal or default.

XVI. That the Alms-people keep their several habitations neat and clean, as well as the court, wash-house and bake-house, garden and out-offices appurtenant

Figure 75 Broadsheet with articles regulating the administration of Stockton almshouses, 1833. Note that Codford landowners are among the Trustees.

Poor Relief

Aside from these specific acts of charity, each parish was responsible for the care of its own poor under legislation initiated in the 16th century and reformed during the 1830s. A little information survives about how poor relief was dispensed in Codford St Peter before the reforms. There was no poor house, but the parish overseers made regular weekly payments to the poor, and to those caring for the sick and elderly. They occasionally paid paupers' rent, and sometimes supplied food, soap, clothing and furniture, as well as paying for medical treatment and medicines and – when all else failed – funeral costs, including shrouds, coffins and the tolling of the passing bell. In return, able-bodied paupers had to work for the parish on tasks such as road repairs.[132]

Statistics relating to the amount of poor relief dispensed and the number of individuals relieved have survived for both Codford parishes between 1776 and 1834. These show the fluctuations experienced in both parishes before, during and after the Napoleonic wars. They also highlight the disparity between the two parishes. St Peter's had far more of its population below the poverty line than St Mary's, and had to spend more per head on relieving them. Several factors seem to have contributed to this problem. Codford St Peter was smaller in area but more populous than its neighbour, a smaller proportion of its families relied on agriculture, its

'We don't want to do any mischief, but we want that poor children when they go to bed should have a belly full of tatoes instead of crying with a half a belly full.' Wiltshire Labourer to Henry Hunt, Radical leader of the time.

From E.J. Hobsbawm and George Rudé, *Captain Swing* (London: Lawrence and Wishart, 1969)

housing stock was of lower quality, and more people lived in over-crowded or insanitary conditions.[133]

During 1830 Codford's parish officials were among the first in the region to face an ugly backlash from the recipients of poor relief. Protest was not only centred on the amount paupers were paid and their treatment by the overseers; it was also aimed at the farmers and landowners responsible for the low wages (for which Wiltshire was notorious) and unemployment that were seen as the root cause of their poverty. One overseer, Thomas Slade Whiting, overheard mutterings of discontent after paying out the weekly dole, and had the ringleader arrested. Another, James Raxworthy, found his house targeted for an arson attack by a disgruntled former employee, William Mussel (*alias* Olden), whom he had accused of dishonesty. Both Whiting and Raxworthy were farmers. Sarah Wheeler, a pauper whose rent was paid by the overseers, set fire to her landlord's outbuildings, and was tried and transported.

Codford was at the centre of the Captain Swing riots in Wiltshire. The riots, which took place through the autumn of 1830, combined demands for higher wages and tithe reductions with direct action such as the destruction of threshing machines. A skirmish took place in and around the river and water meadows at Codford in broad daylight on 25 November 1830. About 300 rioters on their way from Heytesbury came face to face with the yeomanry and constabulary who were taking captives to face imprisonment and trial. No one from Codford was subsequently prosecuted over this incident, but it occurred so close to the village that it is hard to imagine that local people were not involved. Swing letters were certainly received by a farmer in Codford St Peter.[134]

Figure 76 A *Punch* cartoon, published in 1844, commenting upon the Swing riots. 'The house of the rick burner' shows an impoverished labourer being tempted to violence by the devil.

In 1835 both Codfords joined a union of poor law parishes centred on Warminster, and John Ravenhill of Ashton Gifford was elected chairman of the board of guardians which oversaw the union and maintained its workhouses. At first Codford poor continued to receive 'outdoor' relief as before, but, after a new workhouse had been built at Warminster, paupers from Codford were housed there, and set to work crushing bones. In 1843 one turbulent Codford inmate, Praxell Alford Hinwood, smashed the workhouse windows. She also sent abusive and threatening letters to its governor and to Thomas Slade Whiting, who had employed her on his farm. Eventually and involuntarily she was transported to Tasmania, where she died shortly afterwards. Other Codford residents, such as Charles Oliver and his family in 1836, emigrated willingly, and their fare to America was paid from Codford St Mary's poor rate.[135]

Providing Services

Not all the needs of a small community such as Codford can be easily met from its own resources. Healthcare provision in particular, many public services and utilities, and public transport have all fallen outside the scope of parish government. Codford was connected to a mains electricity supply in 1934, but it has never achieved mains sewerage or a gas supply. When eight council houses were built with baths in 1938 there was no mains water; this was installed by the military authorities for their own use between 1939 and 1945, and then taken over and extended in

Figure 77 Overton House, rebuilt in brick for the local surgeon in the early 19th century. It stands next to St Peter's churchyard, probably on the site of a much older house, known as Hungerford House in the 18th century.

1949–51 by the rural district to those Codford residents willing to pay for the connection work.[136]

Health Care Isaac Flower (died 1889) was the first known physician or surgeon to have lived in Codford. From 1835 he resided at Overton House next to St Peter's church, and continued to practise medicine until at least 1876 – not only for Codford's benefit but also as medical officer to the Warminster Poor Law Union. His successors in Codford were G. F. Chadwick, and later E. Winbold Lewis, public vaccinator and medical officer. By this time, in 1905, his efforts were supplemented by the Codford Nursing Association, which continued until after 1945 and the advent of the National Health Service. A general medical practice for Codford is now provided from a surgery in Cherry Orchard.[137]

Coaches and Carriers

The turnpiking of the main road through Codford in 1761, although the work of a private trust, led to improvements which benefited the whole community and in particular made possible the development of coaching and carrying services. Stagecoaches operated through Codford from the later 18th century until the 1840s, probably stopping at the *George Inn*, where the landlord also kept post-chaises for private hire. The eight stagecoaches which passed through weekly in each direction between Salisbury and Warminster in 1795 had risen to 31 in the peak year, 1839, declining to 18 in 1848, and ceasing altogether once the railway was built. They included in 1830 a mail coach, and most coaches called at Codford during the afternoon. Market-day village carriers continued to provide a public service, supplemented from 1914 by a motor van carrying passengers and produce from Chitterne through Codford to Salisbury. Regular motor bus services from

Figure 78 A print of c.1830, showing a stagecoach travelling along a turnpike road.

Salisbury along the Wylye Valley to Trowbridge, and later to Bath, were inaugurated by the Wilts & Dorset company in 1921 and have continued ever since. The first motor car registered in Wiltshire to a Codford resident, in 1904, belonged to a local surgeon.[138]

Mail conveyed by coach would have been handled by the *George Inn*, but by 1841 Codford had a post office, probably operated from the house now called Wellin Cottage. Between the 1850s and 1930s Home Close (formerly Shirley House) was the post office, and mail was routinely taken by handcart from there to the railway station. So busy did the office become processing mail for troops between 1914 and 1918 that a single-storey brick extension was built and an additional pillar box provided. Unlike the Commonwealth troops there was no separate camp post office for British servicemen based in Codford. During the 1930s the post office crossed the road to 74 High Street, and continued there, with another busy period between 1939 and 1945, until after 2000. It was then closed and became 'The Old Post Office', and postal services were transferred to the filling station. A rare George V letter box of *c*.1932 was in use until after 1994, when it was removed and installed in the village hall.[139]

Young Minds

Until the Victorian period education in Codford was somewhat haphazard. The earliest known schoolmaster was Abraham Hayes, who moved from Boyton to Codford St Peter, and taught children at home. When he died in 1683 he had three desks and a cupboard full of books. Not long afterwards, in 1704, John Hinton and Mary Collins both had schools in Codford St Peter's, but the latter was reported for not having the required licence from the church to teach. A century later, in 1808, a charity school at St Peter's was in abeyance because the master was a thief, but by 1835 there were two daily schools in the parish with 24 pupils. In Codford St Mary a private school begun in 1833, a dame school operating in 1859, and an establishment for young ladies in 1867, were all probably short-lived, as nothing more is heard of them.[140]

Sunday schools taught reading and writing as well as religious instruction. The Congregational chapel opened in 1811 with a schoolroom attached, in which Sunday and perhaps daily teaching took place until 1843. In 1835, when a lending library was added to the school, it had 30 male and 40 female pupils. The chapel and schoolroom were rebuilt in 1850, but daily teaching there had apparently ceased by 1859. Following, and competing with, the nonconformist school, St Peter's church had a Sunday school by 1819, and St Mary's opened one in 1832, which was held in a small single-storey building east of and close to the church. In 1835 the two Anglican Sunday schools catered for 39 and 43 children respectively.[141]

Most Victorian villages had schools in place providing elementary education, and associated with either church or chapel, long before such provision became compulsory in 1870. Codford was no exception, but both the resulting schools had somewhat unusual histories. The earlier of the two was built beside the main road by Wadham Locke, owner of Ashton Gifford House, at his own expense in about 1844. It was known as Ashton Gifford school, and for many years it was owned and managed by members of the Ravenhill family. They were Locke's successors at Ashton Gifford House, and they helped out by teaching singing, scripture and reading. Funding was by government grant, voluntary contributions and 'school pence' paid by parents. Any shortfall was made

Figure 80 High Street, Codford St Mary end, looking west, with St Mary's school flanked by the Chitterne brook (left) and Church Lane (right).

Turnpike Trusts

Turnpike trusts were an early form of privatisation. Bodies of trustees were authorised by Parliament to make improvements to specific stretches of roads, in return for which they were permitted to charge tolls from travellers. The trusts also set up milestones and signposts, supervised the statutory road maintenance required from each parish, and employed surveyors and gatekeepers, for whom they built cottages beside the road, known as tollhouses. Originally the barrier at which road users had to pay their toll was a pikestaff, which the toll-collector turned once the payment had been made. Hence the name by which such trusts were known. Most turnpike trusts were set up in the 18th century and were wound up during the 1870s or 1880s, when their functions were replaced by Highway Districts. Apart from new or improved stretches of roads still in use, the most familiar legacy of the trusts' work are the series of milestones along main roads and the occasional tollhouse, often distinguishable by its polygonal shape.

In Wiltshire the earliest turnpike trusts were concerned with portions of the roads between London, Bath and Bristol. They began in 1706, but it was not until 1726 that any roads in south Wiltshire were turnpiked, and most road improvements in the area were undertaken by trusts set up during the 1750s and 1760s. Two important turnpike trusts, based in Amesbury and Fisherton Anger (Salisbury), were authorised in 1761 to take responsibility for long stretches of major roads (including what are now known as the A36, A303 and A360), and both impinged on Codford. The Fisherton trust in 1761 turnpiked the Wylye valley road all the way from Salisbury, via Wilton and along Codford's main street, to Heytesbury, where an earlier trust continued the route to Warminster. The Amesbury trust, as well as controlling the main Exeter road from near Andover to the hill above Mere, also turnpiked the road

Figure B *Upton Lovell tollhouse survives but has lost its porch.*

from Shrewton, through Chitterne, to Heytesbury, which crosses Codford's downland. In addition they controlled the minor Wylye valley road from Little Langford through Wylye and Stockton to 'Cook's House, Codford', which was probably close to where Giggan Street joins the old main road. Why a turnpike trust should be concerned with such an insignificant road is slightly mysterious, but it was probably a ploy to prevent travellers evading tolls by diverting on to minor roads around tollgates. The end of both trusts came within months of each other, in 1870 and 1871.

The Fisherton trust erected metal mileposts along the main Wylye valley road, and several survive. There is one by the playing field fence in Codford and another outside Hillside Café. They also placed metal markers at parish boundaries, probably to ensure that there were no arguments over which parish had to contribute to the maintenance of specific sections of road. A marker survives where the boundary between Codford St Mary and Fisherton Delamere crosses the road by the trackway to Starveall Farm. There were tollgates at Stapleford to the east and Knook to the west, but in 1836 the Knook gate was replaced by a new one, with a weighing house, by the turning to Upton Lovell. The house for the gatekeeper survives, and the weighing house is now a bus shelter.

For further information on sources, see Bibliography.

Figure A *A boundary post on the main Wylye Valley road.*

Figure C *Upton Lovell weighing house, now in use as a bus stop.*

This map shows the principal turnpike roads which served the Codford area.

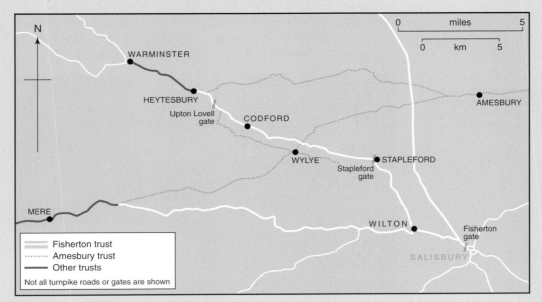

up by the Ravenhills. Only in 1891 was the school brought into the state education system, and in 1900 the managers purchased the building from the former owner's executor.[142]

The schoolroom, 49 by 16 ft, could accommodate 70 children, and there was a separate room for infants as young as three years old. The average attendance in 1864 was 59, and children left school when they reached 12; although at this period the building was also used for evening classes, whose students studied for the same examinations as the day pupils. Fluctuations in pupil numbers were largely the result of changes at other schools. By the late 1860s numbers peaked at 105, but soon fell to an average of 51 when schools opened in Codford St Mary. Sherrington children attended from the 1880s and the school roll rose to 73, but then fell steadily to as few as 22 by 1926. In 1934 it became an infants' school only, taking children from Boyton and Corton as well as from Codford, and its accommodation was reorganised. Although it could accommodate 70 it had fewer than 50 pupils in 1940, but numbers were swollen by evacuees to a total of 76 in 1942, and one class was transferred to Codford St Mary's school. After the war numbers settled to between 33 and 54, and the school closed in 1966, its remaining pupils transferring to Codford St Mary's.[143]

As the 1870 legislation approached, which required communities to provide elementary education, in Codford St Mary the Congregational chapel took the initiative. Its members opened a public day school in the chapel schoolroom in 1869, which was registered under the provisions of the 1870 act. With no school of his own the rector suggested that this become a board school for the children of both Anglican and nonconformist families. But negotiations foundered, probably over questions of religious instruction and church attendance, so that a separate Church of England school was built on glebe land and opened in 1876.

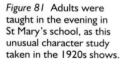

Figure 81 Adults were taught in the evening in St Mary's school, as this unusual character study taken in the 1920s shows.

Figure 82 Codford St Mary school's log book, now deposited in WSRO, recording events in 1888 before and after the Harvest Holiday (24 August – 1 October). School log books were a requirement, under a code introduced in 1862, for schools to be eligible for a government grant. Teachers had to submit them annually to the schools' inspector. They are useful and vivid sources which help build a rounded picture of social life in a local community, providing vital information on matters such as childhood illness, family poverty and infant mortality, as well as the farming year, domestic concerns of parents, attitudes of gentry and clergy, and communal celebrations.

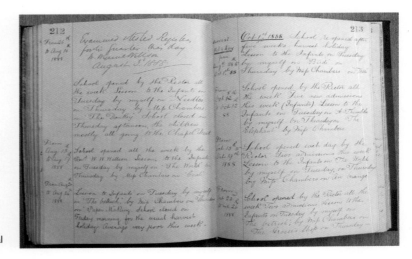

The Congregational school closed three years later and its pupils transferred to the new school or to Ashton Gifford.[144]

Like Ashton Gifford the new St Mary's school derived its income from voluntary contributions, a government grant and school pence, levied on a sliding scale from 3d. to 1d. One qualified teacher was assisted by a monitor, and the school opened with 13 boys, 13 girls and 18 infants. There was one large classroom, with a smaller room for infants, and the building was used for Sunday and evening schools as well as the daily lessons. The premises were enlarged in 1889 to accommodate 124 pupils, and soon children were admitted from other parishes. Absenteeism occurred among the boys at harvest time or when beaters were needed for shooting parties.[145]

After 1900 numbers began to fall, so that in 1913 only 35 children attended the school. But this trend was reversed by 1924, with over 70 pupils, including some from other schools. Older pupils were transferred from Ashton Gifford in 1926, and children came from Boyton and Corton in 1932 when their schools closed. Education was reorganised in 1934. Codford St Mary became a junior school only, with infants attending Ashton Gifford and secondary provision for over-11s at Warminster. As a result numbers fell again, from 67 in 1933 to between 22 and 30 by 1938, but then rose as evacuee children arrived, to stand at 55 in 1943. After 1945 Polish refugee children attended who could not speak English.[146]

As the population in and around Codford rose during the 1950s and 1960s so the school roll increased, and a hutted classroom was added in 1961. With the closure of Ashton Gifford school in 1966 and Chitterne school in 1967 the roll stood at 113 and was predicted to rise to 143 pupils. It was decided to build a new school

Figure 83 Ashton Gifford House from the south, when it was being used as a preparatory school, *c*.1940-1990.

on a site at Cherry Orchard, and this opened in 1971, drawing children from Stockton, Boyton, Sherrington and Upton Lovell, as well as Codford and Chitterne. In 2005 Codford Church of England Primary School federated with Steeple Langford School to form Wylye Valley School. Infants are taught at Steeple Langford, and infants and junior pupils at Codford.[147]

Ashton Gifford House was used as a private school for 50 years between about 1940 and 1990. Greenways, a private preparatory boarding school for boys, rented the house and then purchased it in 1946. The buildings and grounds were modified to provide facilities which included a hobbies room, gymnasium, swimming pool, library and playing fields. In 1949 there were four full-time and six part-time teachers, with 54 pupils, of whom 43 boarded, and boys were admitted as young as five. The standard of tuition was high, and several boys had won scholarships. Although open in 1965, the school had closed by 1973 when the premises were put up for sale. In 1990 they accommodated a residential school for 35 maladjusted boys, aged 11 to 17, but in 1991 Ashton Gifford House was sold and reconverted to a private dwelling.[148]

Joining In

Like most local communities Codford has enjoyed celebrating national events such as royal jubilees, typically with dancing, sports, fireworks and a communal meal. Such occasions are recorded in 1897, 1902 and 1935. Home-grown musical entertainments were provided in the early 20th century by glee singers, bell-ringers and a choral society, and the village has nurtured a strong theatrical tradition. In 1919 a surplus army building purchased as a school extension was named the Little Theatre, and from 1929

Figure 84 Ashton Gifford School, begun *c.*1844, and converted to a private house, 'Moonrakers', after it closed in 1966. It was sometimes referred to as Codford St Peter's school. Traces of a porch facing the street can be seen as well as alterations at the east end.

the Codford Concert Party performed in Codford and surrounding villages. The most abiding and successful theatrical venture has been the Woolstore Theatre and the groups of players associated with it (see Panel 11).[149]

Another focus of Codford's social life is the large modern village hall, opened in 1993, which provides a sports hall, meeting room and licensed bar, with adjacent playing fields. Its predecessor was a tin hut at Broadleaze, originally occupied as a YMCA after 1915, and then by a club called the Red Triangle, which held debates, arts and crafts exhibitions and concert parties. The hut was also used by the British Legion and the youth club; after its purchase for the parish in 1947 it became known as the Codford Club, and housed a weekly cinema for some years. It was demolished when the new village hall was built on land further south.[150]

A football club existed by about 1910 and was re-formed between the wars. A cricket club laid out a pitch in the grounds of Stockton House, and a tennis club was established in the 1930s. All restarted after World War II, and the football club's youth team developed into a youth club. In addition to the football club's first and second teams, cricket and tennis, bowls and badminton are other sporting clubs which now flourish, alongside gardening, Scottish dancing and keep-fit clubs. The Women's Institute, established in Codford in 1924, the British Legion, and an Evergreens

Woolstore Theatre

Codford's village theatre resulted from a society scandal during 1924-5, involving a young adventuress and a retired colonel, whom she married for his money shortly after his first wife had died. Duped but infatuated, Col Ralph Sneyd made two attempts to divorce his new wife, Irene Alexander, for her adultery, and eventually succeeded, but only after being embarrassed in the courts and through newspaper law reports. From a distinguished family (whose seat became Keele University), Sneyd was living in Hampshire during the scandal, but in 1926 he married a third time and escaped to what is now called the Wool House in Codford. His new bride (Dorothy Miller, but known as Stella) enjoyed acting, and as a present for her and her theatrical friends (who included the vicar, Canon Meyrick, and his wife) he fitted out the Woolstore courtyard as a theatre.

From their first production in 1928 the Codford Amateurs, as the group styled themselves, flourished to such an extent that in 1938 they came fourth out of more than 200 entries in a national contest. Plays were curtailed during the war, as the theatre was requisitioned for military use, but resumed in 1948. Although Col Sneyd died the following year and his wife moved away, the Codford Amateurs were allowed to use the theatre until 1955, and continued to produce plays. A separate organisation, the Woolstore Country Theatre Club, was established by Lionel Crawhall, Wiltshire County Drama Adviser, who lived in Codford, for people interested in learning about all aspects of theatre. The Amateurs and the Theatre Club merged in 1964 after the theatre had been purchased by the Amateurs' chairman, Harry Cole, and later sold for £400 to four benefactors on behalf of the Theatre Club.

The theatre had many influential supporters during the 1950s and 1960s, and offered an imaginative programme of plays and events. By the 1970s, however, enthusiasm had dampened and there were problems with maintaining the building. Its resurgence began in the 1980s when an ambitious series of improvements to the theatre – electric heating, piped water, repairs and redecoration – commenced, and this has continued in a spirit of great enthusiasm with a redesigned foyer and auditorium.

In 2000 Karen Johnstone published a short history of the theatre, from which most of these details have been taken. Col Sneyd's folly, which started it all, is alluded to in the history, but is best followed through reports in *The Times*, via the online *Times* digital archive.

Figure A *Group from the Woolstore Theatre with Stella Sneyd in the centre, c.1940s*

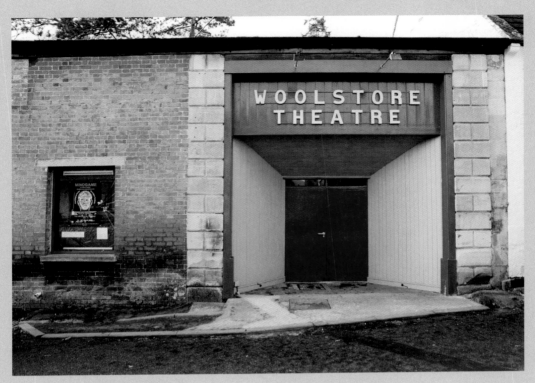

Figure B *Exterior of Woolstore Theatre*

Figure C *Interior of Woolstore Theatre*

Figure 85 As well as
its theatre Codford
has a modern village
hall, opened in 1993,
with facilities for sport,
meetings and relaxation.

Club for elderly residents, formed in 1964, are among the social
clubs for adults which still meet in the village. For children there
was a play area between 1938 and 1950 next to Chitterne Road
(the site was then used for a police house) and later at the playing
fields beside the village hall. Two pre-school playgroups existed
by 1989, and in 2002 there was a parent and toddler group, a pre-
school playgroup – the Codford Caterpillars – occupying premises
next to the primary school, and packs of Wolf Cubs, Brownies and
Boy Scouts.[151]

Chapter 6

Investing in the Afterlife

Until – reluctantly – they united in 1930, Codford always had two congregations meeting in separate parish churches with separate clergy, property and administration. They worshipped the same God, of course, in much the same way, and within the same established church hierarchy, but their histories ran distinct, if parallel, courses. In this chapter the two parishes are described separately up to 1930, but their histories are unravelled in the same order. First, in a section titled 'Patrons and Property' the origin, organisation, funding and property of the church are described. Then, in 'Ministers', the clergy and their officials are examined. Finally, in 'Worshippers', attention is turned to the parishioners who attended church, and those who went elsewhere. The chapter ends by looking at the recent history of religion in Codford, since its two parishes were united.

For much of its history any parish church has been far more than a place for religious worship. Codford's churches have been involved in its social history and local government, their territories have shaped its geography, their clergy have farmed its land, and the church buildings themselves are an important part of its architectural heritage. All these topics are discussed in other chapters.

ST MARY'S PARISH

Patrons and Property

There must have been a church at Codford St Mary long before the first written reference to it in 1282. Not only is the font Norman, but pieces of very early Norman sculpture were found in the walls when the church was rebuilt in 1843, and part of the chancel arch may date from around 1060, just before the Conquest. The owners of what became Codford St Mary manor held the right to present clergy to the living as rectors and owned the rectory and its estate until the 17th century. It is very likely, therefore, that one of their Anglo-Saxon predecessors built the church close to his own home, presumably on the site of East Farm, for his own use and that of his tenants. The impact that such rights could have on the parish is illustrated by the actions of the Mompesson family in the late 16th and early 17th centuries. In 1612 Giles, then lord of the manor,

Figure 86 (left) Tomb of Sir Richard Mompesson (d. 1627) in Salisbury Cathedral. It demonstrates the wealth, status and ambition of a family that provided both patrons and an incumbent of Codford St Mary.

Figure 87 (right) The Mompesson tomb in the south chapel of Codford St Mary's church, moved there in the 19th century. It bears the family's arms and was erected between 1581 and 1620, probably to commemorate Richard (d. 1584).

appointed his brother John rector. John, who remained incumbent until his death in 1646 but who probably lived at his other Wiltshire living, North Tidworth, was responsible for the restoration of the chancel and perhaps for the construction of the grand family tomb which still survives there with two fragmentary effigies (see Chapters 2 and 3). This kind of personal patronage, however, came to an end in 1639, when Giles, who had been forced to sell most of his land in Codford, gave the rectory estate to St John's College, Oxford. Thereafter, up to 1930, the college presented rectors to the living, often from among their own fellows.

Many early churches were dedicated to the Blessed Virgin Mary, so it is likely that the church at East Codford always had this dedication, which became affixed to its parish. A chapel within the parish dedicated to the Holy Cross is mentioned in a single document in 1317, and its story is bound up with that of the Codford hermit (see Panel 12).[152]

To support himself and his household, and to keep in repair the chancel of the church and the rectory house, the rector received all the tithes of the parish. Tithes amounted to one-tenth of the crops grown in the parish, as well as every tenth animal reared, and one tenth of the wool, garden produce, and animal products such as eggs and honey. The living was also endowed with a considerable farm, known as the glebe, which in 1341 included arable, meadow, a dovecot, rents, and pasture for ten draught beasts and 200 sheep.

Figure 88 Mompesson coat of arms from the Mompesson tomb in Codford St Mary church.

Figure 89 View from north-east of St Mary's church in 1804 before the 19th-century restorations.

Medieval rectors may have farmed their own glebe, but in the later 16th and early 17th centuries they leased it to others. In 1672 a small house and garden formed part of the glebe, which the rector rented out. By then, after disputed adjustments, his quota of sheep for pasturing had been reduced to 180, by 1705 it was only 133, rising to 140 in 1763. At this date the glebe consisted of about 25 acres of arable, about three and a half acres of inclosed meadow, an orchard, garden and rickyard.[153]

The descriptions of glebe land, known as terriers, from which such statistics are derived, also give details of the rectory house and its outbuildings. In 1672 it was described as a mansion house, with orchard, barn, stable and pigeon house (perhaps the dovecot recorded in 1341). The 1783 terrier describes the stone and timber house in detail, including its wallpaper and wainscoting, and its thatched stone stable and wooden barn. This house and barn were sold in 1930. The barn has subsequently been demolished but the house, divided into two dwellings, survives.[154]

With their glebe land, tithes and substantial house, the rectors enjoyed a comfortable income and lifestyle. Many such livings came into the possession of medieval abbeys, and after them of laymen, who creamed off most of the income and installed a vicar. In neither Codford parish did this happen, so that when the value of the rectory was reported in 1835 to be £306 and the value of the tithes in 1839 to be £345, the rector was probably earning in excess of fifteen times that of his labouring congregation.[155]

Ministers

Not all St Mary's medieval rectors lived in their parish. Robert de Warenne, rector from 1298 to 1321, obtained permission in 1298, 1301, 1311 and 1312 to attend university for study. William Man, rector from 1436, also served as confessor to Joan of Navarre, Henry IV's queen. Curates probably stood in for them, and in 1394 there is a reference to a curate assisting the resident rector.[156]

Although religious changes at the reformation seem not to have troubled either clergy or parishioners, doctrinal and political turbulence in the 17th century had its repercussions in Codford. John Mompesson, who like other members of his family was a Royalist, observed royal fasts and seldom preached, so that when he died in 1646 he was about to face disciplinary proceedings. His successor, William Creed, an Oxford don, managed to hold onto his livings, at St Mary's and later Stockton, even though he had preached to the king in Royalist Oxford, and been expelled from the university in 1648. With the Restoration in 1660 he was appointed Regius (king's) professor of divinity at Oxford, as well as archdeacon of Wiltshire and prebendary in Salisbury Cathedral. He died in 1663 and was succeeded by another fellow of his college, St John's, one Thomas Edwards.[157]

From a report by his parishioners in 1674 Edwards seems to have been a model clergyman. He lent them his books, rarely left the parish, and carried out all the duties himself, at the correct times and properly dressed. He preached every Sunday, catechised children, visited the sick, baptised ailing infants, chose his parish clerk carefully, and kept the rectory house and barn in good repair. Their high opinion of him was reiterated in 1689, and he served the parish for a total of 35 years, until his death in 1698. Not all his successors were so conscientious. Thomas Smith, rector from 1758 to 1790, was also vicar of Swindon, where in 1783 he was living. His duties at Codford St Mary were performed by a diligent curate, Henry Williams (who also served Stockton and Fisherton Delamere), who catechised children, gave the sacrament at major festivals, and took two services in the church every Sunday. St Mary's last resident rector was Canon C. H. Meyrick, instituted in 1924, who became rector of the united parish, moved to St Peter's rectory, and served both churches until his death in 1951.[158]

The rector had both paid and unpaid officials to assist him. The first parish clerk was John Crouch, in 1654. Twenty years later the duties of the paid clerk, who was chosen by the rector, were said to include taking care of the church and tolling the bells when required. A sexton, appointed and paid for by the parishioners, was first recorded in 1783. Churchwardens were unpaid officials,

Figure 90 Codford St Mary's rectory house. When built in the early 17th century, it was a modest house, unlikely to have been the residence of gentry rector John Mompesson (1612-45).

elected by the rector and parishioners annually, although most held the office for several years, and some for long periods: John Ingram's stint of 27 years (he died in 1785) was easily beaten by Charles Notley (died 1904), churchwarden for 48 years.[159]

One duty of the churchwardens was to report problems to the diocesan authorities, and several such reports, known as present-ments, survive from the later 17th century. In 1662, among other criticisms, no parish perambulation had taken place recently, some chapters of the church bible had disappeared, and other books were missing. They were still missing in 1683, though by 1689 the church-wardens were taking steps to obtain a new bible and rebind the prayer book. The church needed whitewashing, and they confessed that they had not kept their accounts properly. No accounts in fact survive until the 20th century, when there were always two church-wardens, one nominated by the rector, the other by the vestry.[160]

Worshippers

Records say little (apart from some complaints in 1394) about religious observance in the medieval parish, and most of what we know about worship at St Mary's derives from the evidence of the building itself (see Chapter 2). Religious ceremonial increased in drama and elaboration throughout western Europe in the late Middle Ages, and St Mary's was no exception with its richly deco-rated interior and its rood screen separating, and partly hiding, the priestly activities at the altar from the worshippers in the

The Codford Hermit

The Christian religion played a very important role in medieval English society, which respected the calling felt by many men and women to withdraw from worldly concerns and live lives of devotion and prayer. For most this meant the communal life within a monastery, but others practised their religion alone, as hermits. Stray references to hermits survive from all over Wiltshire, and buildings which may have been hermitages survive at Malmesbury, Chapel Plaister near Box, and the Tory, Bradford on Avon. Hermits might have specific tasks, such as maintaining a road or bridge, collecting donations for charitable foundations or maintaining chantries, where prayers were offered for the dead.

In 1317 Codford St Mary's manorial lord, Oliver de Ingham, was granted permission by the Crown to give two acres of land to a hermit, Henry Marsh, where he was to build from new a chapel and somewhere to live. Henry and his successors were to pray daily for the souls of Oliver and his family for ever, and so were to fulfil the function of chantry chaplains. The site of their hermitage was called *Crouchelond*, meaning 'the place of the cross', and their chapel was to be dedicated to the Holy Cross.

The only evidence for Henry the hermit is found in a Patent Roll, one of a series of official documents recording government business. But when Sir Richard Colt Hoare was investigating the history and archaeology of the Codford area in the early 19th century he noticed a group of eight ancient yew trees standing alone on Malmpit Hill above St Mary's, and discovered from old maps that this area had been called Hermitage Hill. At first he was unaware of the Patent Roll reference, although one of his researchers mistakenly told him that the hermit was named in a bishop's register. By the time that Sir Richard's history was ready for printing the patent roll reference had been discovered, and its Latin text was included in an appendix to the book. Later, in 1845, the story was taken up by James Ingram and recently a poem has been published about the hermit.

Codford hermitage is a good example of historical detective work. Despite a false start (the hermit is not mentioned in the bishops' registers for the period, which since Sir Richard's time have been published and are easily searched), the relevant document (the patent roll) is eventually found. The historian then brings together evidence from the document, a folk memory (the name 'Hermitage Hill', which was then included on a printed map of Wiltshire), the old map itself and archaeological fieldwork, to tell us the who, where and when of the story. But is it true? Perhaps Oliver de Ingham obtained permission but never

Andrews and Dury's Map of Wiltshire, 1773, marking Hermitage Hill. This is probably the map that alerted Sir Richard Colt Hoare to the possibility that the yew trees marked the site of the hermitage.

Philip Crocker's map of Heytesbury hundred, for Sir Richard Colt Hoare, 1824. Hermitage Hill is shown, but the position of the yew trees, unfortunately, is not.

carried through his intention to found a hermitage; or perhaps Sir Richard was wrong in his assertion about the yew trees, and they had nothing to do with the hermitage site.

On the other hand, if it is all true, maybe the evidence is telling us more than Sir Richard has deduced from it. The first part of *Crouchelond* derives from an Anglo-Saxon word for a cross, *cruc*, or its medieval equivalent, *crouche*; and the wording of the document strongly suggests that the name was already in use when the proposed hermitage was being planned and indeed determined its dedication. That in turn may imply that a cross was, or had formerly been, on the site. This is pure speculation, but it prompts the search for more evidence. If, from maps or botanical fieldwork, the position of the old yew trees could be determined, then an archaeological investigation could be undertaken to look for the remains of the hermitage and anything else which may have preceded it.

Sources: VCH Wilts 3, 152-3; CPR 1313-17, 661; Hoare Modern Wilts 1(2) 231, 319-20; Ingram 40, 47; C E Mathews, The hermit of Codford St Mary.

James Ingram's translation of the Patent Roll entry, published in 1845. The original, in Latin, was transcribed and published by Sir Richard Colt Hoare.

In English thus:

" Know ye, that we of our special grace have granted and given license, for ourselves and our heirs, as far as lieth in us, to our beloved and faithful Oliver de Ingham, that he may give and assign two acres of land with the appurtenances in East Codford, in the county of Wilts, in a place called Crouchland, which he holds of us in capite, to our beloved brother in Christ Henry de Mareys, chaplain and hermit, to construct anew in that place a chapel in honour of the Holy Cross, and houses fit for habitation, in order to celebrate therein divine service, *singulis diebus*, for the souls of our predecessors, and the souls of the predecessors of the said Oliver, to have and to hold to the said brother Henry and to his successors, chaplains and hermits, who shall there celebrate divine service, *singulis diebus*, for the said souls for ever: And to the same brother Henry, that he may receive the two acres aforesaid, with the appurtenances, from the said Oliver, and there construct the said chapel and houses, and the same hold for himself and his said successors for ever, as is aforesaid, by the tenor of these presents we have in like manner given our special license; the statute for not placing lands and tenements in mortmain notwithstanding; being unwilling that the said Oliver or his heirs, or the said Henry or his successors aforesaid, by virtue of the premises, should be obstructed, molested, or aggrieved, by us or our heirs, justices, escheators, sheriffs, or others our bailiffs or ministers whomsoever. In testimony whereof &c.—Witness the king himself at Westminster this 6th day of June (1317).
By brief under the privy seal."

b This is the French spelling of the name; in many Latin documents we find *De Marisco*, in English, MARSH; a common name to this day.

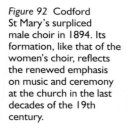

Figure 91 The medieval chalice of Codford St Mary. The stem and foot date from *c*.1500; the bowl is a modern replacement.

Figure 92 Codford St Mary's surpliced male choir in 1894. Its formation, like that of the women's choir, reflects the renewed emphasis on music and ceremony at the church in the last decades of the 19th century.

nave. As elsewhere, most of the medieval fittings, liturgical vessels and vestments were swept away at the Reformation. Remarkably, however, like the neighbouring parish of Wylye, St Mary's retained its late medieval chalice, now displayed in the chapter house of Salisbury cathedral. As later, bells were used to summon worshippers to church, and we know that in the later Middle Ages St Mary's had three. They have all, however, been replaced, in 1582, 1602 and 1615.[161]

The changed atmosphere in which worship took place after the Reformation is reflected in the much plainer building and simpler vestments and ornaments (see Chapter 2). In 1783 not only were the furnishings very simple, but the rector's vestments were limited to a single white surplice. The parish had, however, acquired a new set of communion plate.[162] By the 17th century, a clearer picture of church life emerges thanks to the records kept by the churchwardens. In 1674, for example, they reported that almost all parishioners attended church and behaved well during services and in the churchyard. By 1683, however, there were signs of dissent. Several parishioners refused to take communion or even attend church. One of these, Henry Knight, was described in the burial register as 'an obstinate ignorant fanatique', but not excommunicated; another, Winifred Crouch, was a Roman Catholic who adhered to her religion. A century later, in 1783, the rector admitted that there were only about twenty communicants, although he claimed that there were no dissenters except one, a Baptist.[163]

In fact a meeting of dissenters, known as Independents, had probably begun in the parish a few years earlier, and by 1798

their numbers were sufficient to convert a barn and license it for worship, followed in 1811 by a purpose-built chapel. One of the instigators of the Independent or Congregationalist cause was Benjamin Rebbeck, builder of Ashton Gifford House, and when he lost his estate through debt, William Hubbard, his mortgagor and successor at Ashton Gifford, became a generous supporter of the chapel. Marriages and infant baptisms were taking place there by 1850, when the chapel was enlarged so that, including a gallery, there were seats for 300 and standing room for a further one hundred. Three services were held each Sunday in 1851, and approximate attendance figures when a census was taken were 200 at morning service, 70 in the afternoon and 300 in the evening. In the later 19th century burial services were held in the chapel, although it never had its own burial ground.[164]

By contrast, the parish church was neglected in the early 19th century. At some point a west gallery had been inserted, lit by a dormer window, and this was probably used by the musicians who accompanied services on bass-viol (cello), flute and seraphine (a kind of harmonium). But in 1843, weakened perhaps by the insertion and then removal of the rood loft centuries earlier, the south wall of the church suddenly collapsed, narrowly missing a man working nearby. The Anglican parishioners and rector raised almost £600 by private subscription to rebuild the entire church, apart from the tower, and to construct a new south aisle, under the direction of the diocesan architect, T.H. Wyatt. An organ was installed to replace the musicians, a new communion table was made from the pulpit of an Oxford church (with new plate to

Figure 93 Codford St Mary's women's choir in 1894.

adorn it), and the seating was increased from 120 to 204. Average attendance in the rebuilt church in 1851 was estimated to be 30 to 60 at morning service, and 150 to 200 in the afternoon. The total population of the parish at this date was 390.[165]

The late Victorian worshippers at St Mary's, although probably a minority within the parish, came largely from the wealthier elite. They were able to afford a very necessary second restoration in 1878–9, and make lavish donations which reflected the congregation's high church leanings. These include the carved stone reredos with blind arcading, and matching timber lectern, both installed in 1891, coloured glass for the nave west windows in 1898 and 1912, and for the east window (by Powell and Sons) around 1910. Further communion plate was acquired, and the organ, in poor condition by 1927, was replaced in 1937.[166]

High Anglicanism may have rankled with some worshippers, who therefore swelled the chapel services. Codford's Congregationalists opened a daughter chapel at Wylye in 1860, and continued to prosper despite clashes of personality. Disagreements with his deacons led to the departure of a minister in 1870, and perhaps another in 1876–7 (the 'unfortunate circumstances' were left unexplained). There must have been further problems during the 1880s, when all the pages relating to a particular ministry were torn from the chapel's record book. But in 1897 the Codford chapel claimed to be drawing worshippers from six nearby villages, to the chagrin of the Codford rectors whom they accused of trying to stifle nonconformity. The rector of St Mary's admitted in 1909 that he found the presence of so many dissenters in his parish to be impeding his ministry.[167]

How ineffective the Anglican ministry had become was apparent when troops descended on Codford between 1914 and 1919. The army chaplain worked with the Congregational minister rather than the rector, and so many soldiers attended chapel services that

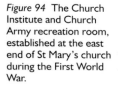

Figure 94 The Church Institute and Church Army recreation room, established at the east end of St Mary's church during the First World War.

Figure 95 Soldiers relaxing in the Church Army recreation room during the First World War.

the gallery had to be strengthened. Religious services, including prayer meetings, were held almost nightly, soldiers helped in the Sunday school, and gave so generously that the chapel no longer needed financial aid. It was perhaps in response to these developments that the Church Army was established in the parish, housed in a wartime hut to the east of St Mary's church. By 1920, however, chapel attendance had reverted to pre-war levels, and its popularity thereafter waned.[168]

ST PETER'S PARISH

Patrons and Property

Like St Mary's the survival of a Norman font and architectural features suggests that St Peter's church is at least a century older than the first written mention of it, in 1291. If the Anglo-Saxon sculpture (see Panel 3), identified as a cross-shaft or an architectural feature flanking an opening, and dated to around 800, is close to its original position, some form of Christian worship or preaching may have been taking place at the site ever since the evangelising era following Aldhelm's missionary activities in west Wiltshire and Somerset. The dedication of the church to St Peter is ancient, and no earlier dedication is known. It became affixed to West Codford manor in the same way as St Mary to East Codford.[169]

The possibility that the site of St Peter's church may be of early religious significance is perhaps strengthened, not only by its position crowning a slight eminence, but also by the fact that the advowson (or right to appoint a clergyman to the benefice) belonged to the owner of Ashton Gifford, whose predecessors might otherwise have been expected to build their church in a more convenient position close to their own and their tenants' dwellings.

Figure 96 St Peter's Norman font with its pyramidal 17th-century cover.

The advowson descended with Ashton Gifford manor,
nominally at least, until 1689, but as the manor after 1327 fragmented into, successively, two, four and three portions, this led to
complications. In such cases it was normal for each part-owner
to present in turn, with the king presenting when the owner was
a minor, but at Codford this led to disputes in 1417 and 1486. In
1689 the portions of the advowson were reunited by purchase, and
then sold in 1713 to Thomas Kellow, whose descendants retained
it until 1821, and used it to present members of the family to the
living until 1786. Thereafter the chosen candidates failed to take
holy orders and so, in 1821, they sold the advowson to Pembroke
College, Oxford, who presented until 1930.[170]

Although the taxable value of St Peter's rectory was reckoned to
be the same as St Mary's in the Middle Ages, its endowment was
actually much less. The rector had all the tithes, but the parish was
smaller, and the glebe, which was dispersed in Codford St Peter and
Ashton Gifford, was only one-quarter the extent of St Mary's. He
had no garden, orchard, meadow or pasture, was only entitled to
pasture a single horse, and he had to maintain at his own expense a
bull and boar for the parishioners' use. From the later 17th century
the glebe was constant at a mere 15 acres (half on St Peter's manor,
and half in Hookland Field, Ashton Gifford) until enclosure in
1810, when it was reduced to about nine acres. In 1839 the tithes
were reckoned to be worth £460, rather more than St Mary's, and
this figure was repeated as the value of the living in 1887.[171]

The rector had a house in the parish in 1608, which he was
rebuilding or extending, as well as two barns. The rectory house

Hungerford.
(B.Hungerford.)

Figure 98 The Hungerford Arms as depicted in *Burke's Peerage*, 1866.

Figure 99 The Hungerford Arms can be seen on a stop on the moulding over the porch entrance. The Hungerfords were patrons of the living from the earlier 15th until the late 17th centuries. They were probably responsible for rebuilding the nave and porch in the 15th century. Their arms and crest were said by Wiltshire antiquary, Richard Colt Hoare, in 1822, to be 'sculptured on the wall near the porch'.

in the 19th century was twice extended and improved, and in 1930 it became the parsonage house for the united benefice. Two small assets to benefit the parish are recorded: a 'Church Acre', formerly in Hookland Field, the income from which seems to have been intended to pay for bell ropes; and a bequest from Thomas King Harding in 1816 towards the upkeep of the church and churchyard.[172]

Ministers

Little more is known of most medieval rectors than their names and length of incumbency. Only two held the rectory for long periods, Gilbert Ode between 1336 and 1361 (who therefore survived the Black Death), and Robert Reyner, for 37 years to 1455. Some stayed only for short periods, resulting in four rectors between 1470 and 1476 and five into the troubled reformation period, between 1544 and 1553. Two rectors were given conditional leave of absence, and had to provide chaplains as deputies; two others appear to have been pluralists, including Thomas Peers, rector in 1512, who was a papal notary.[173]

From the 17th to the 19th centuries most rectors showed remarkable stamina and longevity. John Swayne, rector from 1644 to 1680, must have steered his parishioners unscathed through the upheavals of the civil war, interregnum and Restoration. His successor, presented after a dispute over the advowson, was Charles Wroughton, who survived 48 years, from 1681 to 1729. He was followed by three members in succession of the Kellow family, who had bought the advowson, then a 49-year stint by John Dampier (to 1839), followed by 43 years served by Henry Wightwick (1841–84). A scurrilous poem printed in a local newspaper suggested that he was cured of his gambling addiction by mistaking a blackened chimney-sweep for the devil, after which he preached repentance every Sunday. Wightwick's successor, Douglas Macleane, an eminent Anglo-Catholic theologian and author, was followed in 1915 by another scholar, Edward Denny (died 1928), an authority on the papacy. Both were canons of Salisbury Cathedral.[174]

The rector in 1783, Charles Kellow, lived in the parish and held two services every Sunday, preaching in the morning, and giving the sacrament at the four major festivals to about twenty communicants. Subsequent rectors apparently were all resident. Dampier sometimes employed a curate, but Wightwick carried out all the duties himself, including in 1864 two services each Sunday, and the sacrament four times each year to about forty communicants. By 1909 the rector claimed that there were ninety communicants, that he gave communion weekly and on some saints' days, that he held

Figure 100 Father Douglas Macleane, rector of Codford St Peter 1884–1915. Macleane was a famous alumnus of Pembroke College, Oxford.

two daily services, catechised children, and taught religious instruction in the school.[175]

As in St Mary's, the earliest record of a paid parish official, a parish clerk, is found in 1654, when John Pryor was elected as 'parish register'. Subsequent clerks were described with approval by the churchwardens in 1662 and 1684. Some early churchwardens, beginning in 1662 when there were two, are known from their reports (or presentments), which mostly related to the fabric of the church and state of the churchyard. In 1704, for example, they reported that two of the tower pinnacles had been knocked down by a storm. One duty was to try to resolve disputes over the right to occupy particular seats in church. In 1674 they reported two parishioners 'for strife and contention', and the same seat may have been at issue again in 1713–14. One of the contestants, John Ingram, a tenant farmer, was himself nominated as churchwarden for the following year, and the matter was left unresolved. Behaviour of a different kind was prosecuted by the churchwardens in 1814, when six local men riotously assembled in the churchyard, broke open the belfry door, rang the bells for more than an hour, and behaved loudly and offensively on the belfry roof. The case against them was dismissed in 1815.[176]

In the later 18th century one churchwarden was chosen by the rector and one by the parishioners. In 1857 they were appointed by the vestry, whose membership was small, and they often served for many years, sharing and rotating this and other parish offices between themselves. In the earlier 20th century they were elected at the Easter meeting of the parochial church council.[177]

Worshippers

The medieval worshippers of Codford St Peter appear to have left no historical record, and the first tangible evidence of their expenditure on the church comes in the form of the three bells which they replaced in 1608, 1625 and 1655. Later, in 1671 and 1725, two more were added, perhaps in a spirit of competition with St Mary's. Also in the 17th century a pyramidal font cover was acquired for the church.[178]

Although there were no dissenters reported in the parish in 1676, a few parishioners were staying away or keeping their children away from church during the 1680s, and by 1700 a nonconformist meeting was being held in the house of Thomas Flower. But, unlike St Mary's, this did not evolve into a purpose-built chapel, and St Peter's dissenters presumably ventured over the parish boundary to join the Congregationalists there. In 1783 the rector reported that most parishioners attended church, sent their

Figure 101 The Reverend Ian Duff, former rector of Codford St Mary's and Honorary Chaplain for the ANZAC day service, officiating at the ceremony in 2006.

children to be catechised and their servants to be instructed, but there were some who professed to disregard religion.[179]

Shortly before 1770 all the pews except one were renewed, and a west gallery may have been inserted at the same time. It presumably accommodated the church musicians who were subsequently displaced when a second-hand organ (from Battersea parish church) was installed in 1852. The gallery itself was removed in 1864 as part of a general restoration of the church between 1863 and 1865, for which £1,360 was raised by subscription. It increased the number of sittings from 158 to 223. In 1864 the rector inexplicably claimed an average congregation of 230 (more than the total capacity of the enlarged church), whereas in 1851 only 30 parishioners typically had attended morning service and 93 in the afternoon. The parish population in 1861 was 359.[180]

Subsequent additions and modifications reflected, if anything more than at St Mary's, the high church tastes of patron, rector and congregation. These included coloured glass, a new pulpit, and a series of commissions to the architect F.C. Eden between 1897 and 1912 for communion rails, a chancel screen in late 17th-century style, and a new lectern. The lectern included a special niche to hold a 1617 folio black letter bible given in 1885, which was subsequently damaged in 1916 when drunken soldiers vandalised the church. A churchyard gateway was added, and a hatchment of Prince Leopold, duke of Albany, was placed near the seat he had occupied while living in the neighbouring parish of Boyton. In 1891 his widow presented a brass chandelier to the church.[181]

Church attendance held up in the early 20th century, with more confirmations. Although some nonconformists lived in the parish and the rector reported some tension between them and the established church at election times, relations were generally friendly, and he believed that most were happy that their children received religious instruction from him at school.[182]

COMING TOGETHER

After Edward Denny, rector of St Peter's, died in 1928, it was proposed that the two Codford parishes be united. Although nine-tenths of St Peter's parishioners were said to be opposed to the change on financial and religious grounds, the united benefice was created in 1930, with Canon Meyrick of St Mary's its rector. He moved to St Peter's rectory, kept high-church observances at St Peter's but made St Mary's low church. So as not to cause offence he adopted the practice of bicycling between services from St Peter's to St Mary's so that the breeze would blow the smell

of incense out of his cassock. He died in 1951. The two Oxford
colleges, Pembroke and St John's, which shared the advowson of
the united parishes decided in 1954 that the right of patronage
should be transferred to Pembroke. St Peter's rectory house was
sold in the late 1960s and replaced by a new house in Green Lane.
In 1973 Stockton was added to the benefice, and in 1979 three
other parishes came together to form a group ministry, the Ashton
Gifford benefice. In 1998 the Upper Wylye Team Ministry was
formed to include eight parishes, of which Codford is the furthest
down the valley.[183]

The introduction of low church practices at St Mary's may have
reduced attendance at the Congregational chapel, but it still had
a resident minister living in the manse in 1939. After the war the
congregation further declined, and in 1964 the chapel's defective
roof led to its closure, followed by its demolition as unsafe during
the 1970s. The manse was converted into two private dwellings.[184]

The rector blamed a similar decline in churchgoing on the difficult wartime circumstances, including the black-out, the call-up
of young people, the time demanded for home guard and air raid
precautions duties, and the coldness of the church because of lack
of fuel. Whatever the cause, one effect was financial difficulties. At
St Mary's in 1946 it was decided that churchyard expenses should
be met by voluntary subscriptions instead of charged to the church.
Then during the 1970s two charities were established to assist with
the upkeep of the churches. The Friends of Codford St Peter Church
was registered in 1975, and the equivalent Friends of Codford
St Mary Church in 1977. Between 1996 and 2001 the greatest
expenditure both have incurred has been on repairs to their respective church roofs. In 2002 the old St Peter's organ was replaced by a
restored Regency style Nicholls organ of about 1820.[185]

Chapter 7 Codford at War

Tanks, gunfire, helicopters and camouflaged soldiers are the familiar sights and sounds of Salisbury Plain, and this association of military training and the downland wilderness has been ever-present since 1897. The British army had used Salisbury Plain for set-piece military manoeuvres before this date – notably in 1872 – but three factors came together in the 1890s to bring about its transformation from sheep pasture to battleground. The growing professionalism of army training demanded large, permanent areas for practice, and by the 1870s this demand was outstripping the heathland around Aldershot which had been purchased in 1854. The collapse of the old sheep and corn farming regime and agricultural depression generally meant that downland areas of Salisbury Plain could be purchased cheaply. Furthermore, legislation passed in 1892 as the South African wars were looming enabled the War Office to purchase land for training more easily than before.[186]

Map 20 Land acquisition by the War Office on Salisbury Plain before the First World War.

Land purchases before 1914 all took place in the eastern and central segments of Salisbury Plain, with garrisons at Bulford,

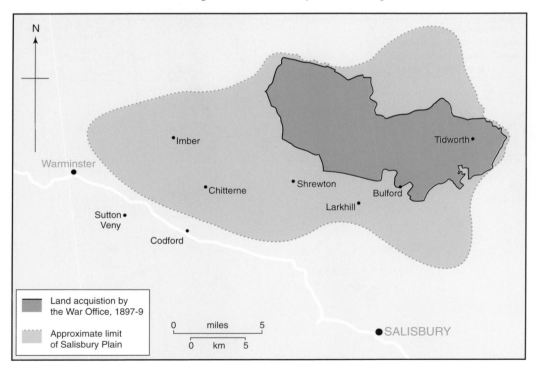

N

• Imber

Tidworth •

Warminster
•

• Shrewton

• Chitterne

Bulford
•

Larkhill •

Sutton •
Veny

• Codford

Land acquistion by
the War Office, 1897-9

Approximate limit
of Salisbury Plain

0   miles   5

0   km   5

• SALISBURY

Tidworth and Larkhill (See Map 20). Codford and the other Wylye Valley settlements were not asked to sell their downland, although much of it was requisitioned for military training during the First World War. Land in the western segment of the Plain, between Shrewton and Warminster, was purchased between 1927 and 1938, and barracks were built on various sites near Warminster during the 1930s. Codford was not directly affected by these purchases, the most dramatic of which eventually led to the evacuation of Imber, some five miles further north, in 1943.[187]

Although Codford was peripheral to the main army training areas during both wars, its easy rail and road access to Warminster and Salisbury made it an attractive location for garrisoning troops. Together with Sutton Veny, some four miles west, it provided the focus for a string of army camps hastily constructed during 1914–15 close to most settlements in the upper Wylye Valley. No fewer than 15 camps and a military hospital were built within the two Codford parishes, linked by a small branch line known as the Codford Camp Railway to accommodate British troops while they undertook training prior to embarkation for France.

Map 21 Map showing the route of the Codford Camp railway and the location of the First World War army camps in Codford, Sherrington, Boyton and Corton.

The transformation of Salisbury Plain to military training grounds, between 1897 and 1914, coincided with the heyday of railway travel and it was inevitable therefore that the railway companies and military authorities should seek to extend the

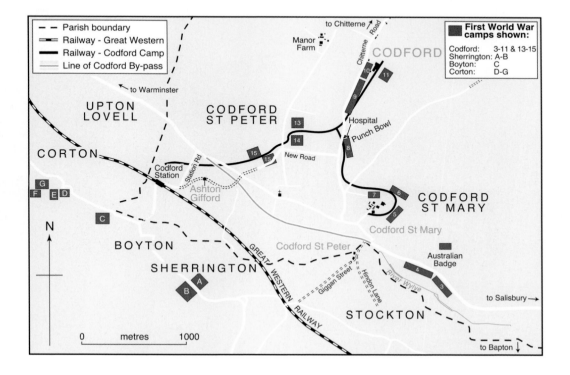

railway network to serve the new camps.[188] The first military line between an existing railhead at Ludgershall to Tidworth opened in 1901, and in 1902 Amesbury was connected by a branch line to the existing station at Porton. This line was extended to Bulford Camp in 1906. After the declaration of war in 1914 five more lines were built, to serve Larkhill and neighbouring camps in the Stonehenge area, as well as installations at Fovant, Porton, Sutton Veny and Codford. All these railways have long been closed although traces of them remain in the landscape (see Panel 13).

Work at Codford began before August 1914 with improvements at the existing station, which included new sidings, a military platform, and a loop line to a new signal box at Sherrington. By October work was in progress on a branch line to carry supplies, personnel and (later) hospital patients from the station to the various camps to the north and north-east of Codford. When complete the line extended to about three miles and its course – avoiding Ashton Gifford and the built-up areas of Codford – can be seen on the accompanying map. At Chitterne Road, north of the New Road junction, the line divided, and a spur headed back to the camps near St Mary's church. The tracks appear to have been lifted after 1918, possibly in 1923, when the loop line at Codford station was removed.

The presence of the troops had a huge impact on the village, where the Woolstore was at least partly taken over, temporary buildings went up and shops and other facilities opened. In July 1916 Codford was chosen as the depot for housing wounded New

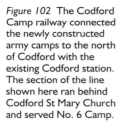

Figure 102 The Codford Camp railway connected the newly constructed army camps to the north of Codford with the existing Codford station. The section of the line shown here ran behind Codford St Mary Church and served No. 6 Camp.

Figure 103 The plantation at Punch Bowl Bottom provided the backcloth for the hutted military hospital taken over for New Zealand casualties in 1916. The complex included general and isolation wards, and shelters for consumptives (tuberculosis patients), as well as quarters for nursing staff and administrative buidings.

Zealand troops during their convalescence. Sutton Veny fulfilled a similar role for Australian troops, although there were Australians at Codford as well. These men, the ANZACs (members of the Australian and New Zealand Army Corps) formed the main element among the troops at Codford but some British soldiers were also stationed there, on their way to the front, including in January 1917 the poet Edward Thomas.[189]

The shifting population of between 2,000 and 4,000 troops and other service personnel (and at times 30,000 nearby) overwhelmed the twin villages, which then had a resident population of just over 500. Existing facilities – the churches, chapel, pub and shops – were augmented by temporary social and commercial buildings, giving Codford's street the feel of a wild west frontier town. Excessive traffic and extreme weather engulfed the place in mud, and its unpopularity with troops was reflected in postcards and poems of the time.

Figure 104 Because soldiers were continually writing home, there was a proliferation of Codford postcards from the period 1914-18. Many examples survive, mostly views of the High Street and buildings. Some correspondents are forthright or sarcastic about the living conditions.

CODFORD, and what we WE think of it.

Some thought it a feather-bed nest,
But Codford will live evermore,
We're not at all fond,
But we're struggling along,
No doubt that to Heaven we'll soar.
At Codford the rain and sleet fall,
And the rats, big as cats, never rest,
And the cupboard is bare,
And Hell cannot compare
With Codford—when its at its best.
There is hardly a girl in the place,
And courting's a thing of the past,
Each night when we pray,
And in chorus we say—
" O ! Lord, let me leave with the draught."
At Reveille, its sad to relate,
Our feet are like great lumps of lead ;
And the language we use,
(We all Codford abuse),
Would put fifty parsons in bed.

It is here that our great soldiers come,
To train on cornbeef and fags
To live a fast life
And forget all the strife,
Of the ways of the cowardly Hun.
I think the great Kaiser's dream,
I'd bet twenty quid to a bone,
He won't give a damn,
I'm sure—that Great Man,
If he can call Codford his own !
Then he'll bring all his great generals down,
Old Hindenburg and Von Kluck,
But I think they'd find out,
They'd developed the gout,
And curse Mein Gott for they luck.
Then peace for ever will reign,
And emblazoned with letters so good,
In History's Book,
We may with wry faces look,
And remember " Codford-on-Mud.
                                          Written by Pte. Whiting.

Figure 105 An annual service is held on ANZAC day, 25 April, to honour the Australian and New Zealand servicemen buried in Codford's military cemetery. In 2006 it was joined by Australian exchange officer Major Andrew Wears (left) and Captain Bill Goldsmith (right).

The camps and hospitals continued in use by New Zealand troops awaiting demobilisation until well into 1919. Many died there, either from grave injuries brought back from the front or from illnesses contracted locally, most notably the epidemic of Spanish influenza which raged in 1918 and 1919. When the ANZACs returned home, they left behind 97 of their number, 66 New Zealanders and 31 Australians, in a military cemetery near St Mary's church. Thereafter, Codford rapidly reverted to its pre-war state, although some of the military and temporary buildings were kept and put to other uses.

THE ANZACS REMEMBERED

The military cemetery in Codford St Mary was established by the Commonwealth War Graves Commission. The second largest of its kind in the United Kingdom, it lies in a peaceful spot by the parish church and its 97 occupants are remembered every year on ANZAC day – that is on 25 April or the Sunday nearest to it – with a dawn service in the cemetery followed by a 'Gunfire Breakfast' of coffee and rum and ANZAC biscuits and a further service at nearby Sutton Veny.[190]

Codford's Military Landscape

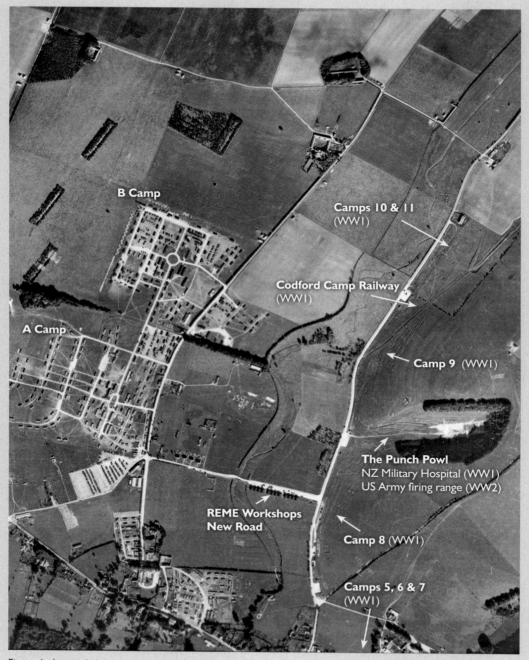

B Camp

Camps 10 & 11
(WWI)

Codford Camp Railway
(WWI)

A Camp

Camp 9 (WWI)

The Punch Powl
NZ Military Hospital (WWI)
US Army firing range (WW2)

REME Workshops
New Road

Camp 8 (WWI)

Camps 5, 6 & 7
(WWI)

Figure A An aerial photograph of the landscape north of Codford High Street taken by the Royal Air Force in September 1945, showing the surviving Second World War army camps and evidence of those from the First World War.

Aerial Photography

Aerial photography can reveal evidence of past landscapes, often very difficult to detect on the ground. Features such as earthworks (banks and ditches), soil marks and crop marks (indicative of buried walls, ditches, etc) or crop marks (indicative of buried walls) are often clearly identifiable. A selected site may be taken at an oblique angle using a hand-held camera, or a vertical photograph may be taken of a whole landscape; both are often invaluable in locating lost sites.

This vertical photograph taken in 1945 shows the landscape to the north of Codford and south of Salisbury Plain, an area noted for military activity during both World Wars. It shows clearly a large number of ephemeral buildings and earthworks that relate to Codford's use as a military camp between 1916 and 1945. The buildings from the First World War were quickly removed following the cessation of hostilities but the surviving earthworks from that period allow various features and camps to be identified. The buildings from the Second World War are clearly visible.

World War 1

There were no fewer than 15 different camps in the landscape around Codford, used principally to house Anzac troops before their deployment to France. Located around and to the north of St Mary's church, the remains of rows of temporary huts can be seen stretching along the eastern side of the Chitterne Road. Also clearly visible are the earthworks associated with the Codford Camp railway that linked the civilian station with temporary halts at the camp sites.

The track running from the Chitterne Road into the Punch Bowl would have served the New Zealand Military Hospital that was established there in 1916.

World War II

Although little survives of the military structures today, in September 1945 the majority of the Second World War camp sites were still largely intact (see Figure A). The RAF photograph shows the buildings and Nissen huts of both A and B Camps in great detail. These camps housed American servicemen as did the Cherry Orchard Camp to the immediate north of the High Street. A substantial tank repair and vehicle depot site can be seen at Bury Mead at the junction of New Road and Green Lane and the former NZ Military Hospital site in the Punch Bowl was adapted for use as a firing range by the Americans.

The remains of a row of wheeled vehicle repair workshops operated by the Royal Electrical and Mechanical Engineers constitute one of the few structures from the Second World War to survive into the 21st century (see Figure B). Situated to the south of New Road, they are clearly visible in the aerial photograph.

Matthew Bristow

Figure B *Remains of REME workshops, New Road.*

CODFORD IN WORLD WAR II

When war returned in 1939 Codford was again chosen as a military garrison for many regiments from the British armed and forces who were joined in 1943 by servicemen from the American Third Armoured Brigade. Camps were built close to or alongside the sites of their First World War predecessors, north of St Peter's and near St Mary's church, and Hindon Lane, which links Codford and Stockton, was requisitioned by the military. Chitterne Road, which was heavily used during the First World War when army camps were built to the east of it, was widened in 1942 and 1943, with

Figure 106 Drummers and buglers march past the Palace cinema in the High Street during the First World War. The open ditch on the left, crossed by small plank bridges, hints at the wet and muddy conditions endured by troops encamped in Codford.

Figure 107 Hut building at Codford during the First World War. The contractors' method of testing the strength of the roof is impressive, if a little foolhardy. Hats were de rigueur.

Figure 108 The unfortunate Mr and Mrs Minty pose for a photograph outside the remains of their house at no.65 High Street after one of Codford's many resident tanks had collided with it during the Second World War.

washing bays and turning places for the up to 200 tanks that were parked along it. The many heavy armoured vehicles which used or crossed the road damaged its surface and deposited hazardous quantities of mud along it. Between 1945 and 1953 the road was reduced to its pre-war width.[191]

The Australian Cap Badge on Lamb Down, which com-memorates the ANZAC soldiers who lived in Codford between 1914 and 1918, is not the only reminder of the presence of allied troops during both World Wars. There are many reminders that Americans were stationed in the parish during the Second World War. None is more evocative than an amateur mural

Figure 109 A mural painted by American servicemen inside the Woolstore, which served as a mess during the Second World War.

painted on the north wall of the first floor of the Woolstore by American Servicemen who used the building as their Sergeants' Club. A dreamy composition depicting the nostalgia for the twin American dreams of skyscrapers and wilderness, it recently has had to be temporarily obscured during the conversion of the Woolstore to apartments.

War art burgeoned during the Second World War, famously seeing an increase in the decorating of aircraft noses and of other machines of war. Between 1941 and 1944, Rex Whistler was stationed at Codford. A renowned and prolific painter from the inter-war years famed for his secular murals, during his time there he transformed the interior of the squalid officers' mess, painting the inside as a Bedouin tent. Sadly this building was destroyed when the Codford camps were dismantled although a similar example of a decorated mess hall survives in the Brighton Museum and Art Gallery. Tragically, Whistler was the first member of the 2nd Battalion Welsh Guards to be killed in action, hit by a mortar round whilst attempting to extricate his disabled tank during the battle for Caen on 18 July 1944.[192, 193]

Although still within living memory and better documented, the Second World War had less impact on Codford than the First. In part this was because fewer troops for a shorter period were based in the village, but it must also reflect the community's familiarity with this transient population.

Coda

Codford, although it is unusual in having been formed from the merging of two settlements focused around two churches at well-separated sites, is in many ways a very typical English village. We hope that the foregoing pages have shown you how much of interest is contained in this particular place, and that by searching through Codford's history you have been brought into contact with significant people and events, sometimes directly, sometimes in more contingent ways. In reading this book, you will have ranged from the Iron Age through to the present – a period spanning over two and a half millennia. Above all we hope that you will have been made aware of how much still lies all around us – in the routeways and buildings, the rediscovered artefacts and the abandoned sites, as well as in the archives, with their written records, maps and collections of visual evidence – old drawings, photographs and the like.

We have tried to show how these diverse materials can be used to produce a vivid and rounded account of an English parish and its history. Local history now involves an understanding of many different disciplines – of archaeology, landscape and settlement, place names and architecture as well as the fundamental task of labouring in the archives. Yet even with all these approaches and resources the modern local historian on his own would have difficulty in putting together a full picture of a place like Codford. Digging out the detail so necessary to bring a place to life requires much specialised knowledge and a huge amount of time and effort. The work of local volunteers in recording and investigating their past has played a key element in this study, bringing to light all kinds of crucial and colourful information to enhance the account. We hope that the results of this fruitful collaboration will inspire more people to get involved in the history of their locality.

In Wiltshire itself the VCH team is currently hard at work in the very north on Cricklade and its nearby parishes. When they have completed this, they will turn back to West Wiltshire, to a volume which will include Codford itself and its neighbours. In all this work local volunteers are already playing a vital and enhancing role, and we very much hope that they will continue to do so.

Endnotes

The following abbreviations are used throughout the endnotes.

Arch J	*Archaeological Journal*
BL	British Library
Cal Papal Reg	*Calendar of Papal Registers*
Cal Pat	*Calendar of Patent Rolls*
Char Com Reg	Charities Commission Register
Cole	Cole, H, *Village history* (typescript in WSL)
DOE List	Department of the Environment, *List of Buildings of Special Architectural or Historic Interest, West Wiltshire* 3 (2) (1987)
Dorset RO	Dorset Record Office (Dorset Archives)
Endowed Char	*Endowed Charities of Wiltshire (Southern Division)* (1908)
Fry	Fry, E A (ed.), *Abstracts of Wiltshire Inquisitiones post mortem 1242-1326* (1908)
Fry and Fry	Fry, G S and E A (eds.), *Abstracts of Wiltshire Inquisitiones post mortem 1625-1660* (1901)
Gover	Gover, J E B (*et al*), *The Place-Names of Wiltshire* (1939)
ICBS	Incorporated Church Building Society
Ingram	Ingram, J, *Memorials of the parish of Codford St Mary* (1844)
James	James, N D G, *Plain soldiering* (1987).
Kelly	*Kelly's directory of Wiltshire*
Non Inq	*Nonarum Inquisitiones* (Record Commissioners)
ODNB	*Oxford Dictionary of National Biography*
OS	Ordnance Survey
Parl Papers	*Parliamentary Papers*
Phillipps	Phillipps, T, *Institutiones Clericorum in County of Wilts from 1297 to 1810* (1825)
PRO	Public Record Office (see now The National Archives)
Reg Ghent	Flower, C T and Dawes, M C B, *Registrum Simonis de Gandavo. . . 1297-1315* (1934)
Reg Langton	Wright, D P (ed.), *Register of Thomas Langton, bishop of Salisbury, 1485-93* (1985)
Reg Waltham	Timmins, T C B (ed.), *Register of John Waltham, bishop of Salisbury* (1994)
Riley	Riley, B, *17th century Wiltshire Quarter Sessions: Presentments of Highways and Bridges* (1995): typescript in WSRO
SDG	*Salisbury Diocesan Gazette*
SJ	*Salisbury (and Winchester) Journal*
Stokes	Stokes, E (ed.), *Abstracts of Wiltshire Inquisitiones post mortem 1327-1377* (1914)
T/A	Tithe Apportionment (in WSRO)
Tax Eccl	*Taxatio Ecclesiastica . . . circa AD 1291* (Record Commissioners)
Thomson	Thomson, S, 'Codford: a farming community in the Wylye Valley' (MA thesis, Bath Spa Univ. 2002)
TNA	The National Archives (formerly the Public Record Office, PRO, and Historical Manuscripts Commission)
VCH	*Victoria History of Wiltshire*
WANHM	*Wiltshire Archaeological and Natural History Magazine*
WANHS	Wiltshire Archaeological and Natural History Society
WBR	Wiltshire Buildings Record
WCC	Wiltshire County Council

WDP   *Western Daily Press*
Wilts Cuttings   Scrapbooks of Wiltshire Cuttings in WANHS Library, Devizes
WNQ   *Wiltshire Notes and Queries*
WSRO   Wiltshire and Swindon Record Office
WRS   Wiltshire Record Society (formerly WANHS Record Branch)
WSL   Wiltshire Studies Library (WCC)
WSMR   Wiltshire Sites and Monuments Record (WCC)
WT   *Wiltshire Times (and News)*
Wyeth *Warriors*   Wyeth, R, *Warriors for the working day* (2002)

Introducing Codford

1 B. Short, *England's Landscape: the South-East* (2006), 119.
2 **Name**: Gover, 164.

Land and Settlers

3 **Forest clearance (general)**: Rackham, O, *History of the Countryside* (1986), 331.
4 **Recent farming**: information from Mrs J Collins, Manor Farm, and Mr G and Mr M Cole.
5 **General**: McOmish, D, *et al*, *Field Archaeology of the Salisbury Plain Training Area* (2002). **Specific**: WSMR ST94SE305; ST94SE624; ST94SE627; ST94SE693.
6 WSMR ST93NE106-8; ST93NE205; ST93NE602-4; ST94SE150; ST94SE200; ST94SE203-4; ST94SE601-10.
7 WSMR ST93NE302-3; ST94SE303-6.
8 **Fords**: P.H.Sawyer (ed.), Anglo-Saxon Charters: an Annotated List and Bibliography (1968), nos. 362, 766; world wide web: anglo-saxons.net.
9 **Name**: Gover, 164; **Stockton**: Whitelock, D. (ed.), *English Historical Documents* I (2nd edn, 1979), number 100; **Area**: Census 1991; *VCH* 15, 235.
10 **Boundary details**: WSRO EA/135; EA/137.
11 WSMR ST94SE401-2.
12 Sawyer, Anglo-Saxon Charters, nos. 362, 766.
13 **Market**: *Cal Pat.* 1247-58, 336;**1608**: PRO CP 25/2/369/6 Jas I Easter. **1760s**: WSRO 906/C/89; WSRO 415/31; WRS 8, pl.5.
14 Above, Sources, Historic Maps.
15 **Early routes**: Ogilby, J, *Britannia* (1675), pl. 32. *VCH* Wilts 4, 254. **Anstlow**: Gelling, M, and Cole, A, *Landscape of Place-Names* (2000), 66-7. **Turnpike**: *VCH* 4, 270; Chandler, J, *Amesbury Turnpike Trust* (1979).
16 **1773 map**: WRS 8, pl. 5. **Hindon Lane**: WSRO F4/250/4. **Green Lane**: WSRO EA/137; OS Map 1:25000, sheet 143, 1998 ed. **Maddington Way**: WSRO T/A Codford St Mary. **New Road**: WANHS Library, sale cat 16.7; WSRO G12/700/1PC.
17 **Market**: *Cal Pat.* 1247-58, 336;**1608**: PRO CP 25/2/369/6 Jas I Easter. **1760s**: WSRO 906/C/89; WSRO 415/31; WRS 8, pl.5.
18 **1582 survey**: WSRO 442/1, 36-44. **1623 survey**: WSRO 490/1522, 13-16v. **1776 survey**: WSRO 906/CC/13. **1773 map**: WRS 8, pl. 5. **1817 map**: OS Map 1:63360, sheet 14, 1817.
19 **Turnpike**: *VCH* 4, 270; WSRO A1/275/1; A1/280/12; Chandler, J, *Amesbury Turnpike Trust* (1979). **Green Lane**: WSRO EA/137; OS Map 1:25000, sheet 143, 1998 ed. **New Road**: WANHS Library, sale cat 16.7; WSRO G12/700/1PC.
20 WSRO 906/C/89-90; Censuses 1811-1881; OS Map 1:10560, Wilts 58, 1889.
21 **Housing stock**: Censuses 1811, 1841, 1891; **George Inn**: WSRO 512/13.
22 **1773 map**: WRS 8, pl.5. **Parkland alterations**: WSRO 682/22; WSRO 512/3; WSRO EA/135; T/A Codford St Peter; OS Map 1:63360, sheet 14, 1817. **Station buildings**: OS Maps 1:10,560, Wilts 58, 1889 ed; Wilts 58NE, 1901 and later eds.
23 **Station**: OS Map 1:10560 sheet 58, 1889 ed. **Sherrington Lane crossing**: WSRO F2/255/69/1. **Engineering works**: Maggs, C.G., *The Bath to Weymouth Line: including Westbury to Salisbury* (1982), 59-63
24 OS Map 1:10560, Wilts 58NE, 1901 and 1926 eds.
25 WSRO G12/132/9,18,20; G12/721/6; WSRO A1/355/413; A1/355/433/1;

A1/355/468/1; A1/355/503/1; WBR B3350; *WDP* 1 June 1993.

26 **1946/7 proposals:** WSRO F4/400/71; *WT* 12 July 1947. **Enquiry:** Wilts Cuttings 32, 49; WSRO F4/200/34; F4/300/69; *Report of Public Enquiry, Codford Bypass* (1987), 4, 6, 42. **AONB:** www.ccwwdaonb.org.uk (10 Aug. 1986)

27 *VCH* 2, 144, 149, 150, 155.

28 **1332 assessment:** WRS 45, 69-71; **1377 poll tax:** *VCH* 4, 308.

29 Whiteman, A, *Compton Census of 1676* (1986), 125.

30 *VCH* 4, 345; Census 1951-2001.

Building the Village

31 *Country Life* 21 Oct. 1905, 570.

32 Where no source is cited, information is derived from fieldwork by Elizabeth Williamson. Thanks are due to Mrs P. Slocombe and Mrs D. Treasure of the Wiltshire Buildings Record, and to Mrs S. Thomson, Home Close, Codford, for their contributions to this section.

33 WANHS Library, Buckler watercolours 8, 17; 8, 57; 8, 70; *WANHM* 27, 273-9; ICBS 03276.

34 **1394:** *Reg Waltham*, 130. **Furnishings:** Ingram, 5-35.

35 WANHS Library, Buckler watercolours 3, 4-5; *WANHM* 27, 273-4; **Hungerfords**, below, Lords and Landowners, St Peter's.

36 Ingram, 34-5; WRS 56, 105; leaflet in church.

37 WANHS Library, Buckler watercolour 3, 4; WSRO D1/61/6/8; 1439/20.

38 **Wyatt's work:** RCHME, *Churches of South-East Wiltshire* (1987), 161; ICBS 02007, 03276; Ingram, 5-35; below, Sunday Best, St Mary's, Worshippers.

39 **Wyatt's work:** ICBS 06065; WSRO D1/61/16/1; 1438/18, faculty 1864; inscription in porch.

40 **Lingen Barker's work:** ICBS 08270; WSRO D1/61/29/9; Pevsner, N (rev. B Cherry), *Wiltshire* (1975), 183. **Later work:** WSRO 1438/19, report 1897; *SDG* 1898, 234; ICBS 14803, ff 12ff.

41 **St Peter's Rectory:** WRS 56, 106; WBR B1281. **St Mary's Rectory:** WRS 56, 103. **Old Manor House:** WBR B1334.

42 **52 High St:** fieldwork by Mrs P M Slocombe. **The Cottage:** *DCMS List*, Codford (1987), 7/61.

43 **Barley Barn:** information from Miss K G Forbes.

44 **Old Manor House:** WBR B1334. **St Mary's Rectory:** WRS 56, 105.

45 **7-8 Riverside:** *DOE List*, 32. **St Mary's Cottage:** WBR B5906.

46 **Rebbeck and Hubbard:** below, Sunday Best, St Mary's, Worshippers; **Locke:** below, Lords and Landownership, The New Order.

47 **Growing together:** OS Map, 6-inch Wilts 58, 1889 ed. **Overton House:** WSRO 906/CC13; 628/32/4; Dorset RO D/FSI box 176a.

48 **Codford Lodge:** information from Miss K G Forbes. **68 High Street:** WBR B1016. **Doughty Lane:** information from Mrs S Thomson.

49 **Home Close:** WBR B9520. **Starveall:** *DCMS List,* Codford (1987), 7/71.

50 *DCMS List*, Codford (1987), 7/39.

51 **Manor House:** WSRO 442/1. **Little Ashton:** WBR B10348. **Victoria Cottages:** WBR B9520, and information from Mrs S Thomson.

52 **Overton House:** WBR B7911. **Chadwick:** *Kelly,* 1889 and later eds. **Manor House:** *DOE List*, 48. **Little Ashton:** WBR B10348. **St Peter's rectory:** WSRO 512/13.

53 **George:** WSRO 490/1529; 512/513.

54 WSRO G 12/721/6; 12/132/16,18

55 **Burford:** WSRO 776/949; *Times* 4 Aug 1950.

56 **East Farm:** *DCMS List,* Codford (1987) 7/45; WSRO 1439/28. **Manor Farm:** WBR B10491. **Rockworth House:** Willoughby, R, *A Gathering of Gardens* (1996).

57 www.ccwwdaonb.org.uk (10 August 2006).

58 DCMS List, Codford, 7/66, 1968.

59 The description is based on a survey undertaken by Sally Thomson, Dorothy Treasure and Clive Carter for the Wiltshire Buildings Record.

60 WRSO 628/47/12 Sale Catalogue 1869.

61 WRSO Codford St Peter Enclosure Award 1810.

62 WRSO Ashton Gifford Enclosure Award 1815; **Land Tax Assessment:** WRSO A1/345/116 Codford LTA.

63 WRSO Codford St Peter Tithe Award 1840;Wool House deeds, 1909.

64 WRSO Tithe Award Codford St Peter 1840; WRSO 628/47/12 Sale Catalogue 1869; OS map 1886.

65 Census return 1861; Wool House deeds, 1929, 1963, 1964, 1974.

66 WRSO Tithe Award Codford St Peter 1840.

Lands and Landowners

67 Mompessons: Richard Colt Hoare, *A History of Modern Wiltshire* (London, 1822), pp. 217, 219, 232.

68 **Codford St Mary:** Fry, 138; WSRO 108/18; 906/CC/1, 3, 7, 12; PRO CP 25/2/888/4 Wm & Mary Mich. **Codford St Peter:** Stokes, 11; PRO SC 6/1050/25; SC 2/208/64, rot. 2; SC 2/208/66, rott. 3-3d; SC 2/208/80 rott. 3-3d; WSRO 490/1536, 1541; 906/CC/4-6, 9.

69 Fry, 236; Stokes, 11, 297-8; WSRO 1976/ boxes 1, 6, 7; 1742/5845; 2057/M5 f.28v; 2057/M12.

70 WSRO 490/1541; 906/CC/2, 4-5; 442/2, p.145.

71 **1524:** PRO SC 2/208/69, rot. 1d; cf WSRO 490/1541; 906/CC/4. **St Mary's and Pounds:** WSRO 906/CC/1,3, 4.

72 **Ashton Gifford pigs:** WSRO 1742/5485; 2057/M12. **St Mary's:** WSRO 906/CC/1,3.

73 **Stewards:** WSRO 906/CC/1-4; 490/1541; PRO SC 6/1050/25. **Haywards:** PRO E 199/47/10; SC 2/208/80, rot. 3d; WSRO 906/CC/4,5. **Affeerors:** Dorset RO D/FSI, box 19 (16 May 1718); PRO SC 2/208/66, rott. 3, 3d; WSRO 906/CC/5. **Sheep reeve:** WSRO 1490/1536. **Gamekeeper:** WSRO 906/CC/2, ff.8, 8v, 10.

Making a Living

74 *VCH* 2, 144, 149, 150, 155.

75 This and two subsequent paragraphs rely on Fry, 236, 452.

76 Stokes, 10.

77 **Crops:** WSRO 906/C/17; WSRO D1/41/4/26. **Codford St Peter field names** (Home, North, Hake or Hook or Hookland, Long Furlong, Cotgrove, Syder or Side Hill): WSRO 442/1; 628/30/4; 906/CC/4; 212B/2037-8; Dorset RO D/FSI. box 126 (lease 1726). **Ashton Gifford field names** (West, Ashton Cliff, West Hill, Swyer, North, Hake): Arundel Castle Muniments TP280 pt.1. **Codford St Mary field names** (Home, Middle, North or Sandells, Further, Braydon, Croft, Low): WSRO D1/24/52/1; 663/1; 906/C/38; D1/24/52/3; 906/C/111/2. For their location see WSRO T/A Codford St Mary.

78 **Demarcation:** WSRO 906/CC/13. ff. 21v-22. **Regulation:** WSRO 490/1541; 906/ CC/1. rott. 2, 4, 6, 7; 906/CC/3, ff. 5, 6; 906/CC/5; Dorset RO D/FSI box 19 (1774).

79 PRO C 2/Eliz. I/E2/61; WSRO T/A Codford St Mary.

80 WSRO 413/322; 663/1; T/A Codford St Mary.

81 **Cattle and pigs:** Davies, J S (ed.), *Tropenell Cartulary* (1908) pt. 2, 82-3; PRO C 143/174, no.13; SC 6/1119/1. **Sheep:** Stokes, 11, 162. **Tax assessment:** WRS 45, 67-73.

82 **1512 and later:** PRO SC 2/208/64, rot. 7; SC 2/208/66, 69-70, 72, 73, 80; WSRO 490/1541; 906/CC/1. **1516:** PRO SC 2/208/66, rott 3-3d. **Sherrington dispute:** PRO SC 2/208/70, rott. 2d, 3; SC 2/208/72, rot. 2d; WSRO 442/2, p.143; 490/1529, ff. 13-13v; WSRO EA 137 implies that the dispute was resolved. **Pound:** WSRO 906/CC/4; EA 137.

83 **Codford St Mary:** WSRO 906/CC/1, rot.1; WRS 56, 103-5. **Codford St Peter:** WSRO 442/2, p.143. **Ashton Gifford:** WSRO 212B/2036.

84 WSRO 442/2, p.143; 1742/5845, 6, 7; T/A Codford St Peter; 490/1529, ff.13v-15.

85 WSRO 442/1, f.43; Arundel Castle Muniments, TP 280, pt.1.

86 **Enclosure**: WSRO EA 135, 137, 164; see WRS 25. **Sales**: Dorset RO D/FSI, box 126, sale cat. 28 Sept 1812.

87 Notley, C, *Childhood Days in the Wylye Valley* (1981), 5.

88 WSRO 906/CC/11, quit rent rolls 1842, 1849.

89 Cobbett, W, *Rural Rides* (1958 ed.), 332; PRO HO 52/20, wilts letter 11 Nov 1832; *Parl Papers* 1868-9 [4202], 13, 525.

90 **Bennett**: WSRO 1942/1; **Ravenhill**: WSRO 663/1.

91 **Chisman**: Declaration in 1855, in possession of Mr H Collins, Manor Farm, Codford St Peter. **Starveall**: WSRO 384/4, valuation 26 Nov. 1844; report 11 June 1845.

92 A Notley's notebooks, in possession of Miss K G Forbes, Bury House, Codford St Peter.

93 WSRO G12/700/1PC; Wyeth *Warriors*, 5, 23; Crawford, T S, *Wiltshire and the Great War* (1999), 76; *Salisbury Times*, 13 Oct. 1916; WANHS Library, Sale Cat 19, 34; PRO MAF 32/33/295.

94 PRO MAF 32/33/295; Wyeth *Warriors*, 118, 188, 190-1; WSRO G12/132/20.

95 PRO MAF 32/33/295; information from Codford farmers, 2002.

96 **1561**: WSRO 906/C/3. **1566**: BL Add. Ch. 73426. **17th century**: Dorset RO D/FSI, box 133, book of customs; WSRO 442/2, 143; 490/1529, f. 13v; 490/1541. **1631-7**: WSRO 490/1541. **Maps**: WRS 8, pl.5; WSRO 415/31; T/A Codford St Peter; T/A Codford ST Mary; OS Maps 1:10560, Wilts 63, 1889 ed.; 1:25000, sheet 143, 1998 ed.

97 **St Mary's mill**: *VCH* 4, 122; Stokes, 220; WRS 52, 133; WSRO T/A Codford St Mary; see also Rogers, K H, *Wiltshire and Somerset Woollen Mills* (1976), 246-7. **Ashton Gifford**: *VCH* 4, 122; PRO C 138/58, no. 4; C 142/774, no. 17.

98 Stokes, 11; PRO CP 25/2/369/4, Jas I Hil; CP 25/2/887/1 Wm & Mary Trin.; SC 6/1148/27; WRS 4, 70; PRO REQ 2/405, no. 105; WANHS Library, Sale Cat 16, 7; 19, 34; WSRO G12/505/4.

99 **Topp**: Fry and Fry, 1901, 145. **Lambert**: WSRO 490/1541. **1656**: Riley, 29. **Alford**: WSRO 682/2. **1839**: WSRO T/A Codford St Mary; T/A Codford St Peter. **mid 20th century**: PRO MAF 32/33/295.

100 *Cal Pat* 1247-58, 336.

101 **1516**: PRO SC 2/208/66. **George Inn**: PRO SC 3/Hen VIII/3915, rot. 13d; *Kelly*, 1848; *Bath Chronicle* 27 July 1787; 22 Dec. 1787; WSRO 512/13. **King's Arms**: Clark, A, *Those were the days* (1933), 179-81; Cole, pt.1, 2. **New Inn**: WSRO 451/426; 906/C/46. **Fleur-de-Lys**: WSRO 512/13.

102 **Tobacconist**: WRS 15, 100. **19th century**: WSRO T/A Codford St Mary; T/A Codford St Peter. **Racehorse training**: WANHS Library, Sale Cat. 15, 14; WSRO 628/48/11; 1439/3, 8, 10. **Weaving**: Thomson, 25-6, table bet. 60-1. **Stockton manor**: *Country Life,* Oct. 21, 1905.

103 Thomson, S *Codford: a Farming Community*, 25; information Mr Kenneth Rogers; Ponting, K *The Woollen Industry of South-West England* (1971) 36; McLaren, WSB *Spinning Woollen and Worsted* (1884) 21

104 **Property**: WRSO A1/345/117 Ashton Gifford LTA; **Wills** :TNA, prob 11/1019 Will of John Raxworthy 1776; prob 11/1841 Will of James Raxworthy; **Connections**: Information Geoffrey Holland.

105 Census returns, Codford St Peter and Codford St Mary 1881

106 Wool House deeds,1929; Rogers, K *Wiltshire and Somerset Woollen Mills,* 247

107 **Emma Dear**: Census Return, Codford 1901; **Alec Dear**: WRSO, Local Directories; WRSO A1/355.

108 **Census returns**: Codford St Peter and Codford St Mary 1841; Corton, 1841-91

109 WRSO 628/47/12 Sale Catalogue 1869.

110 Information Miss Kate Forbes.

111 Wyeth *Warriors*; *Kelly,* 1915 and later eds. to 1939; WSRO G12/505/3; Howell, D (ed.), *Remember the Wylye Valley* (1989), 33.

112 **Wartime**: Cole; Wyeth *Warriors*; Wyeth, *Sterner days* (1995). **1964/1974**: WSRO F14/340/8. **1989**: WSRO F14/180/1.

Friends and Neighbours

113 **Ashton Gifford**: BL Add. Ch. 73426.

114 Davies, J S (ed.), *Tropenell Cartulary* (1908), pt.1, xiv-xvii; pt.2, 109-10, 114-18; WRS 29, 72, 108; *Cal Pat* 1317-21, 572; *WANHM* 37, 7.

115 **East Farm**: WSRO 906/C/3, 10; WSRO 413/322. **Ashton Gifford**: BL Add. Ch. 73426; WSRO 2057/A1/2, ff.11v, 13v. **Codford St Peter**: PRO SC 6/1116/2, rot. 19; WSRO 442/1. f.38v; 490/1529, f.13v.

116 **Hubbard**: WSRO 2755/38; 2755/42. **Locke and Ravenhill**: WSRO 663/1; 512/3-4; *Warminster Herald* 13 April 1878. **Biggs**: WSRO 663/42; T/A Codford St Peter; *VCH* 11, 214.

117 **Bennett**: WSRO H15/150/1, 23; 663/42; *SJ* 7 Oct 1882. **Notley**: WSRO 482/55; information from Miss K G Forbes.

118 **Domesday**: *VCH* 2, 144, 149, 150, 155. **14th century**: Stokes, 11; Fry, 235-6, 452-3; WRS 45, 69-71.

119 WSRO 442/1, 36-44; 442/2, 135-47; 490/1540 ff.43v-45v.; 490/1529 ff.13-16v.

120 Cobbett, W, *Rural Rides* (1958 ed.), 332; *Parl Papers* 1868-9 [4202], 13, 525.

121 Cole, pt.2, 1, 3; PRO MAF 32/33/295; *Census* 1931.

122 PRO SC 2/208/64, rot.2; SC 2/208/66, rot.2; SC 2/208/74, rot. 1d; SC 2/208/79, rott. 1-5d; WRS 49, 157.

123 Riley, 29; WSRO 1438/17, 30.

124 *Endowed Char* 100-1; WSRO 1438/31, 33, 35

125 WSRO 1438/30.

126 WSRO 1438/28-9.

127 *SJ* 8 Dec. 1894; WSRO 1438/41, letter 5 May 1919.

128 **Unwritten law**: Cole, pt.2, 8. **1909**: WSRO D1/56/13, no. 71. **Notley v Hinton**: WSRO 1438/8, 8A; Codford CD-Rom compiled by Gary and Jane Poole.

129 *WT* 12 July 1947; WSRO 2635/2.

130 *Endowed Char*, 103; *VCH* 11, 222; WSRO 1439/6; Char Com Reg

131 *Endowed Char*, 100-8; WSRO L2, Codford; Char Com Reg

132 WSRO 1438/1-2, 35; Chambers, J, *Wiltshire Machine Breakers* (1993), pt. 1, 251.

133 *Parl Papers* 1804 (175), pt.1, 564-5; 1818 (82), pt. 19, 496-7; 1822 (556), supp. app. 5, 745; 1825 (224), supp. app. 4, 267; 1830-1 (83), pt. 11, 444; 1835 (444), pt. 47, 395.

134 Chambers, J, *Wiltshire Machine Breakers* (1993), pt. 1, 19, 21, 67, 251, 257-8; Hobsbawm, E.J., and Rudé, G., *Captain Swing* (1969), 94.

135 WSRO H15/110/1; H14/205/1-2.

136 **Electricity**: WSRO 1439/28. **Water**: Cole, pt.2, 11; pt.4, 5.

137 **Flower**: WBR B7911; WSRO H15/110/1, 125-6, 140; H15/150/1, *passim*; H15/150/2, 98; 1438/8A. **Chadwick and Lewis**: *Kelly*, 1887, 1915. **Nursing**: Cole, pt.4, 4.

138 **Stagecoaches**: Chandler, J, *Stagecoach Operation through Wiltshire* (1980); *Bath Chronicle*, 27 July 1780; *Kelly*, 1848 ed. **Motor van**: Cole, pt 1, 2-3; **Bus services**: *SJ* 13 Aug 1921. **First car**: WRS 58, 69.

139 Willcocks, M, and Jay, R B, *British County Catalogue of Postal History*, 5 (1990), 108; Cole, pt.1, 3; Wyeth *Warriors*, 23-4, 133; Wilts Cuttings 32, 328; information from Mrs S Thomson.

140 **Hayes**: WSRO D1/14/1/1B, no. 51; Thomson, 57-8. **Hinton and Collins**: WSRO D1/54/19/5. 1808: Lambeth Palace Lib. MS 1732. **1835**: *Parl Papers* 1835 (62), pt. 42, 1033. **1859**: *Parl Papers* 1859 sess. 1 (27), pt. 221 (2) , 16; WSRO 2755/38. **1867**: *Kelly*, 1867.

141 **Congregational**: *VCH* 3, 140; Wilts Cuttings 1, 12; WSRO 2755/42. **Others**: *Parl Papers* 1819 (224). pt. 9 (2), 1033; 1835 (62), pt. 42, 1033; Ingram, pl.1.

142 PRO ED 7/130, no. 80; WSRO F8/600/74/1/3/1; 628/19/1.

143 *Parl Papers* 1877 [1882], pt. 67, 410-11; WSRO F8/500/75/1/1-2; F8/600/74/1/3/1.

144 WSRO 2755/38; F8/500/74/1/1.

145 WSRO F8/500/74/1/1-2; D625/2.

146 WSRO F8/500/74/1/2; F8/500/74/1/3/3; F8/600/74/1/3/2.

147 WSRO F8/600/74/1/3/3; www.wylyevalleyschool.org.uk (accessed 28.06.06).

148 WSRO F12/136/2; F8/600/74/1/3/3; 2635/9; PRO ED 109/9176; Wilts Cuttings 12, 339; information from Mr and Mrs R C Hutchins, Ashton Gifford House.

149 **Celebrations:** Wilts Cuttings 10, 81; 12, 339; Cole, pt. 2, 8-10. **Music:** Cole, pt. 1,4; pt. 2, 1-2. **Theatre:** Cole, pt. 2, 2; pt. 2, 5; and see Woolstore Panel.

150 **Village Hall:** *WDP* 1 June 1993; information from Mr G and Mr M Cole, Codford. **YMCA:** Wyeth *Warriors*, 5-6, 143; Cole, pt.2, 2; WSRO 2929/6. **Codford Club:** Wyeth *Warriors*, 143; Cole, pt. 2,3.

151 **Sports clubs:** Cole, pt.2, 1-8; information from Mr M Venning, Brook House, Codford. **Social clubs:** Cole, pts. 2 and 3, passim. **Children's activities:** Cole, pt.3, 10; WSRO F14/180/1; information from Mr M Venning.

Investing in the Afterlife

152 **Early history:** Fry, 138; Wilts Cuttings 13, 217; WSRO D320/1/77, rep. 1959. **Patronage:** *WANHM* 28, 217; Ingram, 40-1., **Mompesson:** *Walker Revised*, ed. A.G. Matthews (Oxford: Clarendon Press, 1948), **Fellows:** *Kelly*, 1867 and later.,

153 **1341:** *Non. Inq.* 155. **Leasing:** PRO C 2/JasI/C23/68. **Glebe:** WRS 56, 103-5.

154 **Terriers:** WRS 56, 103-5. **1930 and later:** WSRO 776/45; WSRO F8/500/74/1/3/3; F8/600/74/1/3/2; WSRO 415/31; WSRO 2499/350/6.

155 *Parl Papers* 1835 (67), 22, pp. 830-1; WSRO T/A Codford St Mary.

156 **Warenne:** Phillipps, 1, pp.1, 18; *Reg Ghent*, 2, pp. 568, 836, 845, 849, 901, 911-12. **Man:** Phillipps, 1, 127; *Cal Papal Reg* Papal Letters 8, 627; *ODNB*. **Benet:** *Cal Papal Reg* 12, 182. **1394 curate:** *Reg Waltham*, 130.

157 **Mompesson:** *ODNB*; Phillipps, 2, 7; Matthews, A G (ed.), *Walker Revised* (1988), 377. **Creed:** *ODNB*; Phillipps, 2, 26; Cox, T, *Magna Britannia* (1738 ed.), 6, 91; *WANHM* 34, 160, 167; WSRO 1439/1.

158 **Edwards:** Phillipps, 2, 26, 44; WSRO D1/54/6/5 no.27; D1/54/12/4; D1/54/13/5. **Smith and Williams:** *VCH* 9, 147; 8, 45; 11, 201; WRS 27, 69. **Meyrick:** *WANHM* 54, 371; information from Revd Ian Duff, Upton Lovell.

159 **Crouch:** WSRO 1439/1. **Duties:** WSRO D1/54/6/5 no.27. **Sexton:** WSRO D1/24/52/4. **Ingram and Notley:** tablets in church.

160 WSRO D1/54/1/4, no. 30B; D1/54/6/5, no. 27; D1/54/10/5; D1/54/12/4; WSRO 1439/18; WRS 27, 69.

161 **Furnishings:** Ingram, 5-35. **Chalice:** WSRO D1/5/2/53; Nightingale, J E, *Church Plate of the County of Wiltshire* (1891), 68-9. **Bells:** Walters, H B, *Church Bells of Wiltshire* (1927-9), 60; *WAHNM* 123, 366.

162 Ingram, 34-5; WRS 56, 105.

163 **1674:** WSRO D1/54/6/5 no. 27. **1683:** WSRO D1/54/10/5. **Knight:** WSRO 1439/1. **Crouch:** WSRO D1/54/6/5 no. 7; D1/54/10/5; 1439/1. **1783:** WRS 56, 105.

164 Antrobus, A, *History of the Wilts & E Somerset Congregational Union* (1947), 15; Stribling, S B, *History of the Wilts & E Somerset Congregational Union* (1897), 51-2; *VCH* 3, 140; WRS 40, 53, 68; WSRO 2755/38, 40, 42; 1439/27; *London Gazette* 7 Sept 1838, p.1947; PRO HO 129/260/3/7.

165 **Musicians:** WSRO 1439/5, note on flyleaf; leaflet in church. **1843 collapse:** Ingram, 34; WSRO D1/61/6/8; Wilts Cuttings 13, 77. **Restoration:** WSRO D1/61/6/8; D1/60/3/35. consecration petition, 1844. **Organ:** WSRO D1/61/16/1. **Attendance:** PRO HO 129/260/3/3.

166 WSRO D320/1/77; D1/61/29/9; tablets in church; *SDG* 1910, 216; Wilts Cuttings 12, 105; 16,242; *WANHM* 21, 356, 370; WSRO D1/5/2/253.

167 **Wylye chapel:** *VCH* 15, 305. **Problems:** WSRO 2755/38. **1897:** Stribling, S B, *History of the Wilts & E Somerset Congregational Union* (1897), 51-2. **1909:** WSRO D1/56/13, no.70.

168 WSRO 1418/2; 2755/39.

169 *Tax Eccl*, 181.

170 **Medieval problems:** *WANHM* 27, 217; Jacob, E F (ed.), *Register of Henry Chichele* (1943), 4, 308; *Reg Langton*, 92; PRO CP 40/897, rot 434. **Beach and Kellow:**

WSRO 473/157; 906/C/113/2-3. **Pembroke College**: PRO CP 25/2/1525/2 Geo IV East.

171 **Medieval value**: *Tax Eccl*, 181; *Feudal Aids* 5, 296; VE 2, 102. **Glebe**: WRS 56, 105-7. **Enclosure**: WSRO EA/135; EA/137. **1839/1887**: WSRO T/A Codford St Peter; Glebe Lands Return 227.

172 **Rectory house**: WRS 56, 105-7; *London Gazette* 20 July 1930, 4714-16; WBR B1281. **Church Acre and Harding**: *Endowed Char* 104; WSRO 1438/17, 29.

173 Most details from Phillipps 1, 31, 53, 107, 145, 160, 163, 165, 170, 180, 187, 211, 213, 215; also *Reg. Ghent* 2, 836, 860; *Reg Waltham* 38, 130; *Cal Papal Reg* 18, 128-9, 342; *Reg Langton* 92; PRO CP 40/897, rot 434.

174 **Swayne**: WSRO 906/C/22; D1/16/1; Phillipps, 2, 21;WSRO 1438/2. **Wroughton**: WSRO D1/18/19; Phillipps, 2, 62, 80, 89; WSRO 1438/3. **Kellow**: Phillipps, 2, 62, 80, 89. **Dampier**: Phillipps, 2, 95; WSRO 1438/8A. **Wightwick**: Wilts Cuttings 16, 91. **Macleane**: *WANHM* 43, 221-3. **Denny**: *WANHM* 44, 272; WSRO 1438/8A; *Times* 17 Nov. 1945.

175 **Kellow**: WRS 27, 79. **Dampier**: WSRO D1/41/4/3; **Wightwick**: WSRO D1/56/7; *VCH* 14, 209. **1909**: WSRO D1/56/13, no. 71.

176 **Pryor**: WSRO 1438/2. **Churchwardens' presentments**: WSRO D1/54/1/4; D1/54/6/5; D1/54/10/5; D1/54/19/5; D1/54/24/5. **1674 dispute**: WSRO D1/61/1/26; D1/39/1/68. **1814 disturbance**: WSRO D1/39/1/75, p.15; D1/41/4/3; D1/54/67.

177 WSRO 1438/17, 29.

178 Walters, H B, *Church Bells of Wiltshire* (1927-9), 60, 296, 300, 304, 319.

179 *WNQ* 3, 537; WSRO D1/54/12/4; WRS 40, 9; WRS 27,70.

180 **Pews**: WSRO D1/61/4/48. **Gallery**: WSRO D1/61/16/1. **Organ**: WSRO 512/13. **1863-4 restoration**: WSRO D320/1/78; D1/61/16/1. **1864**: WSRO D1/56/7. **1851**: PRO HO 129/260/3/7.

181 *SDG* 1897, 117; 1913, 85; WSRO D1/61/48/34. **Lectern**: WSRO D1/5/2/254. **1916 damage**: Wyeth *Warriors* 28-30. **Prince Leopold**: information from Revd Ian Duff, Upton Lovell.

182 WSRO D1/56/13, no. 71.

183 **United benefice**: WSRO 1438/29; *London Gazette* 20 July 1930, 4714-16. **Meyrick**: *Kelly*, 1927; *Crockford's Clerical Directory*, 1947 ed.; WSRO F8/600/75/1/3/1; information from Rev Ian Duff, Upton Lovell. **Patronage**: WSRO 1438/29; D244/1. **Sale of rectory**: WBR B1281. **Group ministry**: *VCH* 11, 220; WSRO D1/166/6, notice 19 Oct. 1979; *Salisbury Diocesan Directory*, 1998 ed.

184 *Kelly*, 1939; Cole, pt 4, 10; *DOE List* 36; information from Miss K G Forbes

185 WSRO 1439/27, 28. **Friends**: Char Com Reg; information from Revd Ian Duff, Upton Lovell. **Organ**: notice in church; information from Revd Ian Duff, Upton Lovell.

Codford at War

186 **Codford at War:** James, N D G, *Plain Soldiering* (1987).

187 James; Sawyer, R, *Little Imber on the Down* (2001).

188 This and the subsequent paragraph rely on James; Wyeth *Warriors*.

189 This and subsequent paragraphs rely on James: Wyeth *Warriors*; Wyeth, R, *Sterner Days* (1995).

190 *DLO News*, 44 (May 2006) 49

191 WRSO EA/164; Wyeth, *Warriors*, 29,118,120; WRSO F4/100/40.

192 Cocroft, W et al., 'Art of War' in *British Archaeology No. 86* (2006).

193 Oxford DNB Whistler, Reginald John [Rex] (1905–1944).

Bibliography and Sources

In what follows we offer an outline of the resources available to anyone interested in following up our work on Codford or in researching the history of any English parish along similar lines. We have used Wiltshire to illustrate the kind of resources available at county level. Increasingly, as finding aids and catalogues are provided online, the Internet provides a convenient and systematic way to search a wide variety of sources both at remote national repositories and libraries and at local record offices and local centres with collections of archival and published material. Besides finding aids and catalogues, a wide variety of sources may be searched, including books and maps, archaeological finds, and material relating to the landscape and to family history.

ENGLAND'S PAST FOR EVERYONE WEBSITE

EPE is developing a highly interactive website which makes available a wide range of complementary material on the project as a whole. Resources include maps and images, digitised documents, oral histories, audiovisual material, databases and commentary on the various places and themes under study. Access to work in each county is by individual county name and the material on Codford can be reached through the Wiltshire section of the EPE site (www.englandspastforeveryone.org.uk).

VICTORIA COUNTY HISTORY

The Victoria County History (VCH), founded in 1899 and originally dedicated to Queen Victoria, is an encyclopaedic record of England's places and people from earliest times to the present day. It is without doubt the greatest publishing project in English local history, having built an international reputation for scholarly standards. Based at the Institute of Historical Research in the University of London since 1932, the VCH is written by historians working in counties across England. The famous VCH big red books, which cover all historical periods, are written county by county from original documents and fieldwork. Introductory chapters of each county set include subjects ranging from archaeology to social and economic history, while topographical sections and whole volumes give comprehensive accounts of each city, town and village, organised town by town and parish by parish. The VCH is currently active in Bristol, Cornwall, Derbyshire, Durham, Essex, Gloucestershire, Herefordshire, Kent, Northamptonshire, Oxfordshire, Somerset, Staffordshire, Sussex and Yorkshire East Riding as well as in Wiltshire. With 14 county sets completed, most counties have at least one volume. More than 240 volumes have been published in total, providing an invaluable resource for everyone interested in local history.

The VCH website (www.victoriacountyhistory.ac.uk) gives details about the VCH project and links to other local history resources. Above all, it provides a list of all published volumes which are still in print, together with links to each county, whether those volumes are still in print and links to the red volumes' publisher, Boydell and Brewer (www.boydell.co.uk). Linked to the main site is a network of county websites. Wiltshire's can be found at www.victoriacountyhistory.ac.uk/Wiltshire and contains news about current work in the county, local events, resources and organisations, VCH Wiltshire volumes, and about VCH staff and sponsorship.

British History Online Many VCH county volumes, including those no longer in print, can be found on the British History Online website at www.british-history.ac.uk. British History Online is a digital library, which was created by the Institute of Historical Research and the History of Parliament Trust and contains some of the core printed primary and secondary sources for the medieval and modern history of the British Isles. These materials can be cross-searched by place, people and selected themes.

OTHER RESOURCES FOR A PARISH HISTORY

The two most important repositories for almost any parish history will be the National Archives and the local county record office. The county is important, because many of the sources for the history of places stem from local government, and are preserved in local record offices and libraries, museums and the collections of antiquarian societies. Many national records, too, use the county as their benchmark. Thus a historian working on a place in Dorset or Somerset, for instance, will follow much the same procedures as a Wiltshire historian, but the names, locations, accessibility and state of preservation of the available sources will all be slightly different.

County Based Resources Almost always the most important archival repository for a rural parish will be the local county records, usually kept at a county record office. Besides this there are usually local studies libraries and the collections and publications of local archaeological, historical and record societies, many of the most important of which were founded in the 19th century and organised on a county basis.

Access to Archives Locally held records can be traced using A2A – Access to Archives – on www.a2a.org.uk. The catalogues in the A2A database have been drawn up over time by archivists who care for the archives they describe. The level of detail provided in the catalogues varies. Some catalogues describe individual files or documents in great detail, including references to people and places mentioned in them. Others only give summary information on each document they describe or provide a brief signpost to a whole archive.

The National Archives (TNA) Formerly the Public Record Office (PRO), it contains in its premises at Kew in west London one of the largest and richest collections of records in the world, ranging in date from the 11th century to the present day. Its holdings form an indispensable resource for anyone interested in the history of his or her parish. The ways in which national government impinged upon local places were manifold, and ensure that its records can provide crucial material relating to a place's people and their occupations, its landowners, church, agriculture, trade, and industry, local government, and education. Much of this will not be available anywhere else. The Public Record Office has published a wide range of calendars, lists and indexes of many of their most important record series. This material can now be searched online at TNA's outstandingly useful website, www.nationalarchives.gov.uk.

The Buildings of England series was begun in 1951 by the architectural historian Sir Nikolaus Pevsner with the aim of providing an up-to-date portable guide to the most significant buildings in every part of the country. The books are a key source for those interested in the history of their locality. Like all volumes in the series, Wiltshire, written by Pevsner in 1963 and revised by Bridget Cherry in 1975, provides an introductory overview of the architecture of the area, followed by a descriptive gazetteer arranged alphabetically by place. Whilst Salisbury Cathedral and Wilton House form two of the book's grand set pieces, the enjoyable diversity of architecture in the county is demonstrated in accounts of rural churches and farmsteads, urban public buildings and recent architecture. The glossary included in each volume is particularly useful to the general reader. The related website www.lookingatbuildings.org provides many other learning materials.

The English Place-Name Society, founded in 1923, publishes a survey of English place-names on a county by county basis. Over 80 volumes have been published explaining the origin and history of the names they study, taking into account the meaning of the elements from which they were created and the topography and environment of the places to which they refer. Based at the University of Nottingham since 1968, the survey now forms a research project within the Institute for Name-Studies there. The Wiltshire volume was published in 1939.

The National Monuments Record Centre (NMRC) is the largest publicly accessible archival resource in England. Located in Swindon, it is run by English Heritage, formally the Royal Commission for Historic Monuments. The material held at the NMR is dedicated to the historic environment, with an unparalleled collection of photographs. Over one million photographs of buildings and the historic landscape are available to be viewed on open access in the public search rooms. The NMR also offers a free basic enquiry service in which their staff will search the archive for specific material following an online or written request by members of the public. In addition to the vast archive of photographs, measured drawings, listed buildings descriptions, survey notes from EH and RCHM work, particulars from estate sales and a large reference library can also be viewed at the NMR. A number of the NMR's collection of archive photographs can be viewed on line at http://viewfinder.english-heritage.org.uk. Although at the time of writing the NMR is undergoing a substantial re-branding, including a change of name, it will remain the premier archival resource for the historic environment.

Images of England (www.imagesofengland.org.uk) is a web-based resource run by the National Monuments Record. Its aim is to present a 'point in time' photographic record of all of the buildings in England which have been afforded listed buildings status. A single image, generated by volunteer photographers, will be web mounted alongside the existing listing description of each building, resulting in a searchable archive of over 300,000 images when complete. A basic search facility is available to all users with an advanced search capability available following the completion of a free registration.

Training and Skills Knowing where to look is only part of the local historian's skill. What to look for, and what it means once found, are the next stages in the process. Shelves of books have been published in recent years describing the techniques for studying local history in general and specific topics. They are to be found in libraries and bookshops, and should be explored by anyone embarking on a local research project. Courses at all levels are offered in local history, in colleges and universities accessible from Wiltshire, or via the internet. And there are bodies within Wiltshire, such as the Wiltshire Local History Forum, and societies in most towns and many villages, which bring local historians together and run events and lectures.

RESOURCES FOR WILTSHIRE

For Wiltshire parishes, the crucial repository is the Wiltshire and Swindon Record Office (WSRO). From autumn 2007 this will form part of a new agency, the Wiltshire & Swindon History Centre, housed in purpose-built premises in Chippenham. Besides the WSRO this will include the Wiltshire Studies Library (WSL), and the staff and records of the county's museums, archaeology and conservation services (all previously attached to County Hall in Trowbridge).

Other important collections are as follows:
- The libraries and museum collections of the Wiltshire Archaeological & Natural History Society at Devizes (WANHS)
- Salisbury & South Wiltshire Museum at Salisbury
- The library of English Heritage's National Monuments Record Centre at Swindon
- The public library local studies collections at Salisbury and Swindon (the latter in new premises in central Swindon from 2008)

At present more information about this material is available on the Wiltshire and Swindon County Archives website and some of the material may be searched through Access to Archives.

The main local serial publications are as follows:
- *Victoria History of Wiltshire (VCH):* 17 volumes (so far) in 18 parts, offering scholarly histories of individual towns and villages, and themed accounts of topics such as agriculture, transport and population. About 75 per cent of the county's parishes have been given detailed treatment. Trace which parishes have been covered on www.victoriacountyhistory.ac.uk/Wiltshire.
- *Wiltshire Archaeological and Natural History Magazine* (WANHM): published regularly since 1854, the series reached volume 100 in

2007. A vast storehouse of useful information about Wiltshire's history.

- Wiltshire Record Society (WRS): Note that until volume 22 (1968) this was the Wiltshire Archaeological and Natural History Society, Records Branch. The society, formed in 1937, publishes editions of important Wiltshire documents, and will achieve volume 60 in 2007.

Other useful serial publications are: *Wiltshire Notes and Queries* (WNQ); *Hatcher Review*; *Wiltshire Folklife*; and *Sarum Chronicle*.

For unpublished sources, footnotes in *VCH* articles are invaluable, and the subject and place catalogues in WSRO should also be checked. Details from many of these now appear online, at www.a2a.org.uk. Gover *et al*, 1939 (see below: Names) is useful in citing documents which refer to specific places.

In the following sections are listed by topic some of the most useful books and published sources for studying a place in Wiltshire. The list is adapted from that appended to John Chandler's *Devizes and Central Wiltshire* (East Knoyle: Hobnob Press, 2003), pp. 263-6.

Bibliography

Goddard, E.H., *Wiltshire Bibliography* (Trowbridge: Wilts Education Committee, 1929) Also Goddard's fuller typescript bibliography on which the published work is based, copies at WSL and WANHS.

Green, R.A.M., *A Bibliography of Printed Works Relating to Wiltshire 1920-1960* (Trowbridge: Wiltshire County Council, Library and Museum Service, 1975).

For work published since 1960 the online library catalogue at WSL should be used, as well as the volume indexes to *WANHM* and other periodicals. There is an exhaustive card index to *WANHM* at WANHS, and cumulative indexes in *WANHM* 8, 16, 24, and 32.

Names

Field, J., *English Field-Names : A Dictionary* (Newton Abbot: David and Charles, 1972).

Gelling, M., and Cole, A. *The Landscape of Place-Names* (Stamford: Shaun Tyas, 2000).

Gover, J.E.B., *et al*, *The Place-Names of Wiltshire* (Cambridge: Cambridge University Press, 1939). This, the standard work, is now very dated, and the following have also been used for specific names:

Mills, A.D., *A Dictionary of English Place-Names* (Oxford: Oxford University Press, 1991).

Smith, A.H., *English Place-Name Elements*, 2 vols. (Cambridge: University Press, 1956).

Boundaries

Sawyer, P.H., *Anglo-Saxon Charters: an Annotated List and Bibliography* (London: Royal Historical Society, 1968). This identifies places with early boundary charters, many of which are described (not always convincingly) by Grundy, G.B., 'The Saxon land charters of Wiltshire', *Archaeological Journal*, 2nd series, 26, 1919, 143-301; 27, 1920, 8-126. The text of charters, including boundary clauses, is available online, at www.anglo-saxons.net.

Youngs, F.A., *Guide to the Local Administrative Units of England*, 1: *Southern England* (London: Offices of the Royal Historical Society, 1979). This dates changes to ancient, civil, and ecclesiastical parish boundaries, but without maps or detailed descriptions. For 19th- and 20th-century changes the footnotes to the parish population tables in *VCH Wilts* 4, 339-61 can be useful.

Communications

Jervoise, E., *The Ancient Bridges of the South of England* (London: The Architectural Press, 1930).

Margary, I.D., *Roman Roads in Britain*, 3rd ed.(London: J. Baker, 1973).

Timperley, H.W., and Brill, E., *Ancient Trackways of Wessex* (1965), should be taken with a pinch of salt. Documentary references to early roads have been collected by Grundy, G.B., 'The ancient highways and tracks of Wiltshire, Berkshire, and Hampshire, and the Saxon battlefields of Wiltshire', *Archaeological Journal*, 2nd series, 25, 1918, 69-194.

For roads, canals and railways, the articles in *VCH Wilts* 4, 254-93 are invaluable. Information about turnpike trusts can be found in local record offices. In some cases the trust's own records have survived, and the Wiltshire & Swindon Record Office holds a minute book for the Fisherton trust, covering the years from 1819 to 1836 (WSRO 2491/1), and letters and accounts relating to the Amesbury trust, covering 1788 to 1810 (WSRO 377/4). Other records were preserved by the county authorities, including financial returns relating to each trust, and the printed local acts of Parliament which gave the trusts their authority to operate. Maps are another important source, as well as auction catalogues produced to sell off the trusts' assets when they were wound up. A good summary of Wiltshire turnpike trusts has been published in *VCH Wilts* 4, 256-71.

Buildings

Pevsner, N., and Cherry, B., *Wiltshire: The Buildings of England*, 2nd ed., (Harmondsworth: Penguin, 1975).

Department of Culture, Media & Sport, Lists of buildings of special architectural and historic interest. Most of Wiltshire was relisted during the 1980s, and a bound set of the resulting lists (known as 'greenbacks') with key map is in WSL. List descriptions are available on the Images of England website (see above).

For medieval chapels J.E. Jackson's article in *WANHM* 10, 253-322 is still worth consulting.

Rogers, K.H., *Wiltshire and Somerset Woollen Mills* (Edington, Wilts: Pasold Research Fund, 1976).

Stell, C., *An Inventory of Nonconformist Chapels and Meeting-Houses in South-West England* (London: H.M.S.O., 1991). Dates of pre-1852 nonconformist chapels and their precursors are generally found in an edition of meeting-house certificates, WRS 40.

The Anglo-Saxon Sculptured Stone: Principal sources: Cramp, R., *Corpus of Anglo-Saxon Stone Sculpture 7: South-West England* (2006); Swanton, M., in *Anglo-Saxon Studies in Archaeology and History* 1, 1979, 139-48; Leslie Webster, 'Aedifica nova: treasures of Alfred's reign', in *Alfred the Great*, ed. Timothy Reuter (London: Ashgate, 2003), 79-103, esp. 88-9; *The Making of England. Anglo-Saxon Art and Culture AD 600-900*, ed. Leslie Webster and Janet Backhouse (London: British Museum, 1991), no. 208.

Landscape and Geology

Barron, R.S., *The Geology of Wiltshire: a Field Guide* (Bradford-on-Avon: Moonraker Press, 1976). This should be used in conjunction with the relevant sheets of the British Geological Survey on Ordnance Survey 1-inch base.

Geddes, I., *Hidden Depths: Wiltshire's Geology and Landscapes* (Bradford-on-Avon: Ex Libris Press, 2000).

Archaeology

McOmish, D. *et al*, *The Field Archaeology of the Salisbury Plain Training Area* (Swindon: English Heritage, 2002).

Wiltshire Sites and Monuments Records, maintained by County Archaeologist, Wiltshire County Council. This should be used in conjunction with *VCH Wilts* 1, parts 1 and 2 (Part 1 is the gazetteer compiled by L.V. Grinsell), and the annual summaries of archaeology and fieldwork in WANHM.

Historic Maps

Andrews J., and Dury, A., *A Map of Wiltshire* 1773 (facsimile edition in WRS 8).

Ogilby, J., Britannia, I (1675).

Other early printed maps of Wiltshire, notably Greenwood, 1820, are reproduced in WRS 52.

Ordnance Survey, 1-inch first series. Most of Wiltshire falls on sheets 14 (1817), 15 (1811), and 34 (1828). Convenient facsimile editions were published by Harry Margary in 1981 and 1986.

Ordnance Survey, 6-inch first series. Wiltshire sheets were surveyed *c.*1880-*c.*1890. Original sheets in WSL and WSRO.

Most manuscript maps in WSRO, including tithe, enclosure, and estate maps, of various dates, 16th-19th centuries, should be examined where relevant, including copies of maps held elsewhere.

Population

Thorn, C., and F., *Domesday Book: Wiltshire* (Chichester: Phillimore, 1979). Also, for Domesday and the Geld Rolls, *VCH Wilts* 2.

Editions of tax lists and assessments have been consulted for the following dates: 1332 (by D.A. Crowley in WRS 45); 1334 and 1377 (*VCH Wilts* 4, 294-313); 1524–5 (by Sheail, J., *The Regional Distribution of Wealth in England as Indicated in the 1524–5 Lay Subsidy Returns*, List and Index Soc, special series 28, 1998, copy in Trowbridge (WSRO); 1545 and 1576 (by G.D. Ramsay in WRS 10).

Whiteman, A., *The Compton Census of 1676: a Critical Edition* (London: Oxford University Press for the British Academy, 1986)

Population tables, 1801–1951, in *VCH Wilts* 4,339-61. Subsequent decennial totals are to be found in 1961–2001 Wiltshire census reports, and in census-derived publications by Wiltshire County Council, held in WSL.

Land Ownership

The range of sources which must be examined by anyone researching a manorial descent is very large, and includes documents held in both national and local record offices, and privately. Many of the principal series have been published, including the *Calendars of Patent Rolls* and *Close Rolls*, *The Book of Fees, Feudal Aids* and *Abstracts of Feet of Fines*. Most sources for population listed above are also relevant, and genealogical sources such as *Burke's Landed Gentry* and the *Complete Peerage* provide vital information about individual owners. The sources for Codford's manorial descents, summarised in this account, are recorded in detail in tables placed in the Wiltshire section of our website, www.englandspastforeveryone.org.uk. They will also be published in a forthcoming volume of *VCH Wilts*. The important sources include:

Rotuli Hundredorum, 2, 230-81 (London: Record Commissioners, 1812–18).

The 1316 Nomina Villarum is printed in *WANHM* 12, 1-43.

Abstracts of Wiltshire Inquisitiones Post Mortem, 23, 37, 48 (London: British Record Society and Devizes: WANHS, 1901–1914). Covers the period 1242–1377, 1625–49.

Summaries of Wiltshire enclosure awards and tithe apportionments by R.E. Sandell in WRS 25 and 30.

Miscellaneous

Aubrey, J., and Jackson, J.E., *Wiltshire: The Topographical Collections of John Aubrey* (Devizes: WANHS, 1862).

Gomme, G.L., ed. *Topographical History XIII of Warwickshire, Westmorland, and Wiltshire* (Gentleman's Magazine Library, 1901).

Grant, R. and Poole, E.H.L., 'Wiltshire Forests', *VCH Wilts* 4, 391-460.

Hoare, Sir Richard Colt, *The History of Modern Wiltshire*, 6 vols (London: John Nichols and Son, 1822–1843.) This covers only the southern half of Wiltshire.

Hobbs, S. ed., *Wiltshire Glebe Terriers 1588–1827*, WRS 56.

Kelly's directory of Wiltshire, various issues, 1848–1939.

Richardson, J., *The Local Historian's Encyclopaedia* (New Barnet: Historical Publications Ltd, 1974) 232-69, lists of market grants, markets and fairs, derived from a not wholly accurate government report of 1889. A better list in available online, at www.history.ac.uk/cmh/gaz.

Smith, Lucy Toulmin, *The Itinerary of John Leland* (London: George Bell, 1906-1909).

Watts, K., 'Wiltshire Deer Parks', *WANHM* 89, 88-98.

Index

NOTE: Places and subjects relate to Codford unless otherwise stated. Italics denote a picture or picture caption.

Picture Credits

The author and publisher would like to thank the following for permission to reproduce their material. Any infringement of copyright is entirely inadvertent and accidental. Every care has been taken to contact or trace all copyright owners. We would be pleased to correct in future editions any errors or omissions brought to our attention.

New maps were drawn by Cath d'Alton (Maps 1, 2, 3, 4, 19, 20, 21 and Panel 10) and Alan Fagan (Maps 8, 9, 10, and 11) using Ordnance Survey 1st edition maps © University of London.